To: April

Hey!. He's no sugar shane mosely
but
He Will Do !! ;)

Merry Christmas

♡
Britt

TIKI

TIKI

MY LIFE IN THE GAME AND BEYOND

BY TIKI BARBER

WITH GIL REAVILL

SIMON SPOTLIGHT ENTERTAINMENT
NEW YORK   LONDON   TORONTO   SYDNEY

SIMON SPOTLIGHT ENTERTAINMENT

An imprint of Simon & Schuster

1230 Avenue of the Americas, New York, New York 10020

Copyright © 2007 by Tiki Barber

All rights reserved, including the right of reproduction

in whole or in part in any form.

SIMON SPOTLIGHT ENTERTAINMENT and related logo

are trademarks of Simon & Schuster, Inc.

Manufactured in the United States of America

First Edition 10 9 8 7 6 5 4 3 2 1

Library of Congress Cataloging-in-Publication Data

Barber, Tiki, 1975–

Tiki : my life in the game and beyond / by Tiki Barber with Gil Reavill.—1st ed.

p. cm.

ISBN-13: 978-1-4169-3843-9

ISBN-10: 1-4169-3843-5

1. Barber, Tiki, 1975–

2. Football players—United States—Biography—Juvenile literature.

I. Reavill, Gil, 1953– II.Title.

GV939.A1B3647 2007

796.332092—dc22

[B]

2007021941

To my wife, Ginny, for always being by my side and for bearing our two wonderful sons.

To my mom, Geraldine, for her motivation and inspiration, and for (every once in a while) whipping our butts and being firm in her discipline, which made me always want to do the right thing.

I love you both.

CONTENTS

TIKI

FORTY-TWO STEPS

Every run from scrimmage tells a story. Every run has a beginning, a middle, and an end.

I've been running with a football for more than a decade and a half now, since the early 1990s, when I played alongside my twin brother Ronde with the Cave Spring High School Knights football team in Roanoke, Virginia. We were teammates at the University of Virginia, too. For the whole of my professional sports career, I was a running back for the New York Giants in the National Football Conference (NFC) of the National Football League.

Running with a football is a specialized skill. Not everyone can do it. So I want to give you an idea of what it feels like.

Beginning, middle, and end. Pick a run, any run. I'll show you the beginning, middle, and end.

Well, maybe not *any* run. Some would make extremely short

stories, one-word smack-down poems. Let's pick a running play that is more of a full-length novel, one that also happens to be one of the best TD runs that I have ever made.

I'll break it down, stride for stride.

December 17, 2005. Giants Stadium in East Rutherford, New Jersey. Our opponents were the Kansas City Chiefs, with their explosive running back Larry Johnson, then just coming into his own in his third season in the league.

The day had high clouds and was cool, with the temperature hovering around forty degrees. A wind out of the west had kicked up earlier, sweeping across the synthetic FieldTurf at the stadium, but by kickoff it had died to a whisper. Perfect football weather.

This was my season. I was playing for pride ("Play proud" is the two-word blessing my mother Geraldine sends Ronde and me on every single one of our game days), I was playing to win (the Giants came into the battle with the Chiefs with nine wins and four losses, in the hunt for the play-offs), and I was playing for my dear departed friends and mentors, Wellington Mara and Bob Tisch, owners of the Giants, both of whom had passed away in the previous six weeks.

I took all those reasons with me to the line when we broke huddle near the end of the first half, a little under three minutes left in the second quarter. The Chiefs were ahead by a field goal, 0–3. We were injury-depleted and had a lot of guys playing nicked. I remember feeling a powerful sense of determination, a calm kind of euphoria. We were behind. I could not, would not, allow the score to stay that way.

Our offense, behind quarterback Eli Manning, had the ball on Kansas City's forty-one yard line. The always steady Eli, who has never uttered a single curse word in the huddle in the three years I've played with him, called "Forty/Fifty Slide East on Red." That meant Eli would hand off to me and I would follow a pulling guard around the right side.

That's not the real name of the play, which is more of an I-could-tell-you-but-then-I'd-have-to-kill-you secret, since the Giants don't change their nomenclature all that often and I wouldn't want our calls to get too public.

As he always did, Eli also called two additional plays, in case the Chiefs altered their defensive set or he saw something that would require him to "check off" or audibly change the called play once he scoped the opponents at the line of scrimmage. One of the checks was a quick (a short pass) and the other was a pitch to me for an off-tackle run on the left side.

I didn't much like the idea of the second check. An off-tackle run to the left would lead me straight at Kendrell Bell, linebacker on the Chiefs' right-side post, a photon-fast Pro Bowl perennial, college shot-putter, and former Pittsburgh Steeler who gobbled up running backs for breakfast. Part of the reason I've been successful at my job is that I know enough to avoid punishing tacklers like Kendrell Bell at all costs.

Whatever happened, whether I ran right or left, Jim Finn would be helping me—"Finny," my fullback, a bulldozer-blade of a blocker who would blast away any tackler in my path.

As we broke huddle, the noise from the 78,000-plus fans swelled in intensity, increasing from sixty decibels, say, the sound of heavy traffic, to more like one hundred, just below a kickoff roar. I inhaled and caught the familiar smell of game day, a sweet mix of autumn air, liniment, and sweat.

The beginning.

Time spiraled down, collapsing as it always does as the center approaches the ball. My heart rate climbed. A team physician could have told you that it increased from its normal sixty beats per minute upward past eighty.

I lined up in I-formation six yards behind Eli, who stood surveying the defense with his 305-pound center, the bodyguard-samurai-bullet-stopper Shaun O'Hara. My respiration rose and then steadied, as if in tune with the mounting screams from the stands.

Shaun screamed louder than the fans, yelling, "Ninety-nine," identifying the key K.C. defender, and Eli echoed him, also shouting, "Ninety-nine."

Shaun went into his crouch; Eli cocked his head slightly to the left so I could hear him and then checked the play to the off-tackle left. "One Taco West, Twenty-Thirty Veer."

I would be heading straight at Kendrell Bell.

Eli began his cadence. In the huddle he had said "on four," meaning the snap would come on the fourth number in the series. "Seven, fifteen, forty"—Shaun would hike the ball on the next count—"two."

The time between the snap and the whistle in professional football has got to be the most compressed, heightened reality this side of military combat. It is a zone beyond thought. I didn't think, *Well, right now Eli will swivel 180 degrees and pitch the ball back to me and I will follow Finny off my left foot.*

It's not that way at all. I don't think. I act. Everything—breathing, body movement, mental processes—becomes automatic.

Eli got Shaun's snap, turned right, and made a single yard-long stride away from the line, so that he was back to the forty-five yard line by the time of his second half step. He pitched the ball to me, two yards behind him. The football sailed within a foot of Finny, who was already booming forward toward the line.

I took my first stride off my left foot, crossing my right leg toward the left side, thereby alerting Bell and his Chief cohorts, who were watching me and Eli like hawks, keying off our movements. I cocked both arms out to receive the ball.

A pitched football from Eli Manning is not a shrinking-violet kind of thing. It's definite. Hard. The ball came at me perfectly. Eli didn't spiral it, but tossed it lengthwise, so that it presented its fattest part to me. I broke off the blocks to meet it. In the midst of my second stride of the run, my right hand pushed the ball up into the basket of my left arm, snug against my bicep.

The moment I take possession of the ball, I become prey. The eleven predators on the Chiefs defense, weighing in at more than a ton (2,741 pounds to be exact, according to their official listed weights), are every ounce bent on my total obliteration.

People talk about quick feet, balance, and speed as ideal ingredients for a running back, but for me the most vital element might be sniper-quality vision. I am not aware of doing it, but I've seen telephoto shots of myself during a run, and my eyes are open so wide they appear unnatural.

I'm taking everything in. I resemble nothing so much as an antelope feeling the hot breath of the lion. The difference being that instead of running away from the predators, I have to run directly at them, an antelope heading straight for the pride.

Right away I saw a problem. The first predator, Chiefs defensive end Jared Allen, had penetrated four yards into our backfield. Giants veteran Bob Whitfield, our offensive tackle on the left side, adjusted quickly. Instead of firing off the line, he stood Allen up and pushed him outside. On my third stride I had a decision to make. I had to figure out a way to get around Allen and not lose my fullback.

I didn't linger over it. I made a stutter-cut to the right, choosing the inside, then veered back left (strides four and five) and came within an inch of Whitfield's firmly planted left cleat as I blew past him and Allen toward the line.

Finny had been there before me. There was daylight. Well, what the sportscasters call "daylight" anyway, but for me it's always getting eclipsed, closing down, about to go dark. I felt like I was running directly into white Chiefs jerseys. With a couple yards still to go to the line of scrimmage, I was cut off on my right by Kansas City defensive end Eric Hicks, rampaging in from the other side.

On my left, sure enough, Kendrell Bell. Number 99. I hunched, protecting the ball, preparing to get hit, and picked up speed. I knew from elementary physics that the best way to bust a tackle is not to shrink from it, not to act on your self-preservation instincts—Slow down! Danger! You are about to hit a wall! Slow down!—but rather to accelerate. Counterintuitive, I know. But it works.

Again, I wasn't puzzling out physics just then. My impulse to accelerate in the face of a tackle was automatic by now, ingrained by years of training, coaching, and experience. Momentum and speed carried me. Finny banged Bell just enough to slow him down, and with my sixth stride I was at the Kansas City forty-one. All that trouble and toil just to get to the race's starting line.

Beginning, middle, and end. The beginning was over. I now entered the middle of the story, the place where novels and movies and oftentimes football runs die a miserable death. I was still braced by Hicks and Bell to my right and left, and about to ram into Jeremy Shockey straight ahead of me.

Shockey. The guy is unbelievable, always running in overdrive, slamming it, jamming it, blowing up the playing field. He's well-celebrated as a go-to pass receiver. For me, he's a kick-ass blocker and the dynamo that lights up the Giants.

Right at that moment Shockey was stacking up not one, not two, but three Chiefs, linemen and linebackers, stopping them in their tracks with a little help from Giants guard Rich Seubert. They all piled together across my path like those concrete walls at which they hurl crash-test dummies.

It didn't matter. Bell was right on top of me. As I broke forward across the forty yard line in my seventh and eighth strides, I could see him to my left out of my peripheral vision. Both of his arms were forklifted straight out, inches away. They looked as long as Yao Ming's. He had me.

Then he held up.

It was inexplicable. Just one of the strange things that can happen in the violent chaos of a gridiron. I've seen 340-pound humans explode upward toward the sky like birds, untouched footballs change direction in midair, quarterbacks bear-hugged and bookended by a pair of defensive ends somehow manage to emerge unscathed. Nothing I see on a football field could surprise me anymore.

But Bell did. By which I mean that somewhere deep in my brain as I made my eighth stride of the play, a neuron fired that registered the strangeness of an All-Pro linebacker who had me virtually in his grasp, only suddenly to pull up and let me go by. It wasn't a complete thought. It didn't register at the time. I didn't even remember it until later, watching film.

So I was past him. Chiefs defensive end Eric Hicks was the first to make contact with me on the play, a lunging push from behind that actually helped me in my cut to the left around the crash-test wall of bodies. In the midst of a run I'll take any help I can get from any source at all.

I was free.

Strides nine, ten, eleven.

Like some lethal seagull, the Chiefs free safety Greg Wesley sailed airborne at me on the thirty-five yard line, smashing his right forearm into my right bicep, a karate-chop blow. Wesley could have ended my run at a modest six-yard gain, but he was just a step behind. Sorry, dude. Wrong angle. See you later.

Strides twelve through twenty brought me to the sideline, my middle-story goal; when you hug the sideline, you know where the bullets are coming from. Aside from the infamous instance of Ohio State coach Woody Hayes darting out from the sidelines and punching an opposing ball carrier in the throat, usually you're safe from that side.

I picked up my downfield bodyguard, the towering wide receiver Plaxico Burress, who wrestled aside a Chiefs cornerback and then came along with me for the ride. You might know Plaxico as an incredibly acrobatic receiver unjustly robbed of Pro-Bowl status, but as a running back I most of all respect him for his excellent, artful blocking.

It all turned Three Stooges on me then. At the twenty-five, I had to pause and actually wait for about a nanosecond.

It happens more often on a run than you might expect—a

moment where your best move is to pull up. You have to wait for your blocks to set. Plaxico and I performed what amounted to a comic square-dance do-si-do, exchanging places so he could stop Chiefs strong safety Sammy Knight. Plaxico flung Knight across my path like a piece of luggage and went on to deal with a Kansas City cornerback. As in an old-time Keystone Cops movie, everyone crashed into one another and fell down at the twenty yard line.

Except me and Plaxico. I was free again. I had to propel Mr. Burress out of my way (excuse me, sir) and outrace the previously disposed free safety Greg Wesley, but strides thirty through forty-one were long, ground-gulping gains.

With my forty-second stride I crossed the goal line.

Beginning, middle, and now the end.

This one had a happy, Hollywood ending.

Touchdown.

And all of it happened in the snap of a finger. Only fourteen seconds on the game clock. But as football wives and all the fans can attest, gridiron time is the most relative measure there is. It sure didn't seem like fourteen seconds to me. It felt like an instant, and it felt like forever.

"When you sit with a nice girl for two hours, it seems like two minutes," said Albert Einstein. "When you sit on a hot stove for two minutes, it seems like two hours. That's relativity."

I had just spent fourteen seconds on a hot stove next to a nice girl.

We never trailed again, and more importantly, we won the game, 27–17. I did what I always do when I score a TD. I blew a kiss. To my family, to the fans, to the Almighty who allowed me to play this amazing, brutal, exhilarating, childish, transcendent, ultimately American game of football.

THE NEXT STAGE

The four of us walked onto a soundstage at NBC studios in New York and took our places in captain's chairs set up in front of the assembled media. Butterflies fluttered in my stomach. This press conference would be a turning point in my life, and I would be lying if I said I wasn't a bit nervous.

February 13, 2007. Jeff Zucker, the president and CEO of NBC Universal, was there, and Steve Capus, president of NBC News, as well as the legendary Dick Ebersol, chairman of NBC Sports.

Facing us in the audience were reporters from the *New York Times*, the *Daily News*, and other print outlets, as well as broadcasters from all over, many of them people I knew from my time with the Giants. Sitting down in front was Matt Lauer, host of the *Today* show. We had become friendly over the years, having encountered each other at charity events. He was one of the people I most admired professionally and most wanted to learn from.

This was my new life. My new, post-football, post–New York Giants life. We were here to announce my future role as a *Today* show correspondent and sports commentator for NBC. Playing football—which I had done since I was eight years old and which helped put me up on the stage with heavy hitters such as Zucker, Capus, and Ebersol—was now behind me.

Amid the bright lights and the reporters' questions, I wanted to enjoy the moment. It was a culmination of what had seemed, sometimes, like an impossible dream. I had set my sights on *Today* from the beginning of my broadcasting career, way back when I had my first radio show on WCBS.

Yes, I had played football for ten years with the Giants, and before that for four years in college, and before that in high school. In my mind, though, being a football player never defined me. I always wanted to branch out, expand my horizons, surprise people.

Be careful what you wish for. As exhilarating as the moment was, it was also like stepping off the end of the Earth for me. Would I find my footing or go into free fall? Playing sports had sustained me, centered me, occupied me for more than two decades, ever since I was in grade school. I was pumped for the challenge, excited about doing something new, but there was also a small voice in the back of my mind, saying, "How can I make this work?"

There was something else, too, another personal concern. For the first time in my life, really, I was doing something different from my identical twin brother, Ronde. The two of us gestated together, were born together (he seven minutes before me), took our first steps together, and went to the same grade school, junior high, and high school, where we played football together. When it came time for us to go to college, we entered the University of Virginia together, where we also played football on the same team, he in the defensive secondary, me as a tailback.

We both joined the National Football League the same year. We almost wound up on the same team, but in the end were drafted to two different ones. During our professional careers, we both went to Pro Bowls, the last one being the last professional football game of my career, just three days before the NBC press conference, on February 10, 2007.

Ronde has chosen to continue on with football as a star of the Tampa Bay Buccaneers. Our paths would diverge for the first time in our lives. One of our closest connections, which stretched but didn't break in 1997 when I was drafted by the Giants and Ronde by Tampa, would finally be irrevocably broken. I was stepping onto the high wire without my usual safety net.

"On those days when you're not feeling so well," cracked NBC's Steve Capus at the press conference, "we'll call Tampa Bay and get your brother up here."

When it came time for questions from the assembled reporters, I felt as though I were on *This Is Your Life*, reliving the history that got me to that point in time. Beyond the *x*'s and *o*'s to life, liberty, and the pursuit of a TV contract. Tom Pedulla of *USA Today* wanted me to reflect on my career as a New York Giant.

"My time with the Giants was phenomenal," I began, in the "safe generalization" mode I knew so well from countless interviews with reporters. "I had a lot of ups and a lot of downs. A lot of boos and a lot of cheers. That time shaped the person I am. It gave me a thick skin, and it gave me resilience."

No one recalls that my time as a Giants running back almost ended before it began, that I had to reinvent myself just to be able to take the next step. Yes, there were times when I was getting booed in Giants Stadium. In my last year, the fans chanted my name. But I remember getting booed, and how much it hurts.

"These last couple of years in particular have been a dichotomy in some ways," I went on. "I became an all-star player, I became one of the elite players in this league, but at the same time the grind started to take its toll on me, and the principles of our head coach started to take their toll on me, and so I started looking for the next thing."

There it was. A minor little news scooplet that I let slip out in front of a phalanx of hungry New York media people. I hinted at the truth: If Tom Coughlin had not remained as head coach of the Giants, I might still be in a Giants uniform.

In a sense, it was thought out. I knew enough about the New York sports media to know that anything I said about Coughlin would get played up in columns and news stories the next day. As of this press conference, I was morphing from reported to reporter. I needed to make a little splash. My new NBC career would get more coverage this way.

Some folks can play the press like a pipe organ. Donald Trump comes to mind, Madonna, Bill Clinton, a few others. I was a piker compared to them, but I knew that if you want the media to write about you, you have to give them something to write about.

It's not like I was saying anything that I wouldn't say to Tom Coughlin's face. Coach Coughlin is a disciplinarian. He has a one-size-fits-all coaching philosophy, treating every player on the roster the same, pushing them all constantly, physically and mentally.

But in the last years of my career, one-size-fits-all didn't fit me. I'd arrive at Wednesday practice still hurting from getting beat up the Sunday before. Coughlin would rag on me for going half-speed. Even more than the quarterback, a running back takes a pounding during games. Especially a back with a role such as I had with the Giants, where I was either rushing or blocking on every play.

I wasn't some greenhorn rookie. I knew the game. I knew my assignments. For a running back, I was old. Ancient. I had done the job for ten years. I could not live up to Coughlin's demands anymore.

It didn't matter. Coach Coughlin treated me as though I had just stepped off the bus. I don't blame the guy—that's just the way he is. An old-school Lombardi type of coach.

But the NFL is changing. It's all about specialization now. Coughlin would virtually have to get a personality transplant to approach the game in the way I'm suggesting—the way it's approached by coaches in other franchises around the league.

I've heard former San Diego head coach Marty Schottenheimer quoted as saying he saved his star back LaDainian Tomlinson from getting beat up in practice, so that L.T. would be fresh for Sunday. There is a realistic hierarchy in place on other teams. You approach your most productive players a little differently, in order to continue getting the best out of them in every game. It just makes sense.

I understand the opposite argument. Every player is equal. Treating some players as "more equal than others," to use a George Orwell phrase, would hurt team cohesion. It's Coughlin's right to approach the game that way, just like it's my right to walk away.

Tom Coughlin's coaching method, his one-track, single-focus

mind, his one-size-fits-all training regimen weren't the only factors pulling me away from football and toward *Today*. Tom Coughlin didn't pull the plug. But he certainly gave it a tug.

The press conference announcing my new career continued. We broke up for individual one-on-one interviews. In a few of those I was, predictably, taken to task for my Coughlin comment ("Giants Will Miss Tiki, Not His Mouth" read one headline the next day). Reporters asked about my future, but they also asked a lot about my past, what had led me to this, why I wanted to change my focus so decidedly.

This book is in part an answer to those questions. It's a ridiculous thing, I know, for a thirty-two-year-old to publish his memoirs. But at the same time I have traveled an amazing journey that a lot of people will find interesting. I've gone from being raised in semi-rural Virginia to holding a high-profile job in television. I accomplished an arduous evolution from being an ordinary performer in my chosen profession, football, to being a standout.

I hope that this book will inspire others in their journeys. But I also hope to memorialize and honor the people who helped me along the way.

My life is all about relationships. I've met amazing, inspiring people, sometimes because they've been my teammates, and sometimes just by happenstance, because I've been in the right place at the right time. They have given me enormous input toward making me a successful person.

I would never fool myself into believing I've done everything on my own. I've always had good people around me who believed in me, motivated out of love, or perhaps because it was in their best interest to make me better at what I was doing. Their motives didn't really matter to me. They helped me.

As much as detailing the ins and outs of professional football, as much as taking you past the sidelines and onto the field to give you the view from inside the huddle, those two questions—how I did it, and who helped me—represent what this book is about.

How do we persevere in the face of adversity? How do we shut out the chorus of negativity and nastiness to put one foot in front of the other and just keep going?

We find a way to put our hearts into it.

It's not as simple as it sounds, and success actually involves a lot of different elements. You can't just say, "I'm going to put my heart into it," and magically reach your goals. There's a lot of work, discipline, and character that goes into the process. But I learned one thing for certain from my football career. Heart is an essential ingredient to success.

Success and happiness come into play when we perform a single act: stepping up. That's it. That's the marker for success and happiness that psychologists from Abraham Maslow on down have determined. I encountered Maslow in Psych 101 when I was at UVA. He was a groundbreaking American psychologist with the innovative idea to study not the lives of mentally ill people (as most psychologists did before him) but of success stories, people like Frederick Douglass, Eleanor Roosevelt, and Albert Einstein, finding out what made them tick. Maslow helped develop the theory of self-actualization, and he said that we're most happy and successful when we progress, get better, move forward. When we step up.

The National Football League is a lot more bookish than one

might imagine. Everyone is feverishly grasping for an edge, and a lot of people have come to recognize that the true edge in any sport comes not simply from physical conditioning. Being in top physical form is necessary but not sufficient in a professional football league where everyone, all 1,440 players who make up the active roster, is constantly working out, bulking up, and refining their already elite physical presences.

No, the true edge in the NFL comes not in the objective, statistical zone of the physical—What's your time in the forty? What do you bench press?—but in the more slippery, more subjective realm of the mental.

That's why a lot of people read, coaches especially. They are looking for hints, clues, secrets. The quest leads them into strange nooks and crannies of literature.

Coach Jimmy Johnson's favorite book was *Flow*, by Mihaly Csikszentmihalyi. From it, Johnson took a lesson about the crucial difference between happiness and pleasure. I can get pleasure from eating a good veal scaloppine at Primola, for example, one of my favorite restaurants in Manhattan. But that pleasure doesn't equal happiness, and it sure doesn't mean success.

"To be happy," Johnson says, "I've got to be challenged, I've got to accomplish things, I've got to have some sense of satisfaction and achievement."

A business bestseller enjoying great currency around the NFL recently is called *Good to Great*, by Stanford University's Jim Collins. The book's three-word title encapsulates perfectly what I was trying to do for my whole NFL career. It expresses a goal that a lot of us have, not only NFL players, but everyone who is serious and ambitious about life.

If we want to be happy, if we want to be successful, we have to find a way to step up. And to do that, we have to find a way to go from merely being good—taking our place among the mass of people who do their jobs, proceed through their lives competently, and achieve acceptable results—to rise above that level and become truly great. As a friend of mine used to put it, to make a big splash, you can't just tread water.

How do we achieve success and happiness?

By stepping up.

How do we step up?

By finding a way to go from good to great.

How do we do that?

That question has always been my central concern, on the football field or anywhere else. I was exposed to the whole idea of stepping up very early on. Two of the most important people in my life started me on my journey, one by her example and the other by his pure competitive spirit.

TIKI INTERVIEWS TIKI

Q You've been a professional athlete for the whole of your adult life. What makes you qualified to work as a broadcaster?

A I've never defined myself strictly as a football player. I've always focused on other things, even while I was playing ball. I've worked for a long time as a broadcaster, starting out with late-night radio and early morning news. I've put in my time and I've earned the respect of my peers.

THE KNIGHTS

All my life I've been determined to be different from everyone else, to take people's expectations and turn them on their heads. Maybe the urge to be singular comes out of the fact that I am an identical twin, similar in so many ways to my brother Ronde. Maybe that's all the conformity I'm ever going to need.

Identical twins aren't really totally identical. Ronde and I have different fingerprints, different body markings. But we share DNA, and my sons and Ronde's daughters are, genetically speaking, half siblings rather than cousins. We come from the same egg. Although we've grown into markedly different adults, we're in essence the same person. In more ways than one—biologically and emotionally—Ronde and I are as close as two human beings are ever going to get in this world.

As an identical twin, I always keeps tabs on other identical twins

I encounter in the news. In 2006, for example, the president of Poland appointed his identical twin as the country's prime minister. There are more than a hundred million of us worldwide, but the only identical twin I know very well is my own. He is my first friend, my double, my soul brother, the guy who always has my back. We bunked in the same room growing up, and we shared a dorm room in college.

My "me" always contained a "we." Of all the friends I've had throughout my life, of all the people who've influenced me, not one of them can touch my brother. When I see my own sons, who were born twenty-one months apart and are very close, I see me and Ronde as kids.

I love my brother, but I've always wanted to best him in everything we tried to do together. Not in a malicious way, but simply in a pure-hearted, proud-of-each-other way. He feels the same level of competition, and we accept that feeling as a natural part of who we are. He was always the better athlete. I knew it and he knew it. I was the better student. He knew it and I knew it.

But because he was better, because he was one step ahead of me, I felt determined to become a better athlete in order to approach Ronde's level. He knew he was better than me already, so he tried to stay a step ahead. Same thing with academics. Our competitiveness pushed us to excel.

April 7, 1975, at Montgomery Regional Hospital in Blacksburg, Virginia. He showed up first, a few minutes before me. My mother named him Jamael Orondé Barber. The first two names mean "firstborn son" in Swahili. I came into the world after him, kicking and squalling and raising such a fuss that my mother named me Atiim Kiambu Barber: "fiery-tempered king."

That was just like my mom, to give us names we had to live up to. Actually, when I said Ronde was the most influential person in my life, that's not the total truth, since we were both equally shaped by our indomitable mother, Geraldine Barber-Hale.

Look up that word "indomitable" in the dictionary, and the definition reads "impossible to subdue." And while there isn't a picture of Geraldine, there *should* be. One of her favorite sayings is: "I'm not one of those people who believes you go through life being afraid to live."

The fact that Ronde and I took her as our role model and inspiration made us all the closer as brothers, all the more identical as twins.

It was touch and go there for a little while. We came into the world three weeks early, as four-and-a-half-pound preemies. We spent the first three days of our lives in incubators. Our pediatrician didn't hold out much hope for healthy, normal childhoods.

"They'll probably never play contact sports," the doctor told Geraldine.

For the first years of our lives, any body temperature change would affect both me and Ronde, sending us into seizures that were terrifying for my mother.

As Mom headed out to work one morning to her job at Virginia Tech, she was about to leave us with a babysitter when she saw Ronde going into a seizure. Naturally, she freaked out, dialing the phone for the local hospital. By the time she got through, I had gone into a seizure too.

"Please be calm, Mrs. Barber," the nurse on the phone said. "Which twin is in seizure?"

"Both of them," Geraldine replied.

We always did do everything together, Ronde and I.

After that episode, our pediatrician reiterated his earlier warning. "Remember, now—they aren't going to be playing any contact sports."

Somehow, Geraldine wasn't intimidated by what the doctor told her. The seizures ended when Ronde and I passed our fifth birthday. And even though we were both shy and tended to hang out by ourselves all the time, pretty much to the exclusion of others, Mom pushed us to go out into the world.

Mom always told us she felt sorry for the babysitters, since they never knew which of us was which. She admits to making that mistake once and only once, when she inadvertently nursed Ronde twice instead of each of us in turn.

"I wondered why you were howling," she told me.

I was always howling. As an infant, I lived up to my fiery-tempered name. That was one of the main ways my mother used to tell us apart. If one twin had his mouth open, pumping out the decibels, it was probably me.

I grew up in a single-parent household in what was then semi-rural Virginia. It could have been an impoverished, hardscrabble life. I sure saw plenty of that around me growing up. But because of my mom's energy, her purpose, and her spirit, my brother and I wanted for nothing. If we weren't exactly middle class, my mother provided us with an uncanny illusion of being so.

She did it by working harder than I have ever seen a human being work, and that includes everything I've seen on the football practice field. Day after day, year after year as we were growing up, Geraldine worked two jobs, sometimes three, to give us everything we needed.

Later on in life, when reporters or acquaintances who didn't know me tried to characterize my background as "poor," I had to beg to differ. Ronde and I never went without. Geraldine's success as a mother represented an incredible triumph of determination over reality.

She spanked us, but not often. She held the threat of a spanking over us more than the reality of it. The life lessons she communicated came from her example, but she did repeat over and over the value of education.

"Brainpower," she called it, and said that once you had it, no one could take it away. She warned us about gifts from others, that it was better to work for something yourself than to take it as a hand out. Behind both these lessons lay the core values of independence and self-reliance.

A few times, our limits actually turned out to be strengths. Money was tight enough around the house that Geraldine made a rule: If you sign up for a sport with a registration fee, you can't drop out. You're committed for the whole season.

That rule kept Ronde and me in athletic programs when our first impulse might have been to quit. It represented an early lesson in perseverance.

Geraldine taught us to be independent, and inevitably we turned that lesson back on her. When we were in fourth grade, Ronde and I sat our mother down in a family council and proposed a new world order. There's two of us, we told her, and only one of you. We all should get equal votes. It's not fair that you can overrule us.

She responded with a line that we joke about even today. "When you make more money than me, then you can tell me what to do."

Ronde and I had a lot of freedom. We were always out on our own, cruising on our bikes. When I was twelve, I took a header at

a construction site, flipping my bike into a thirty-foot-deep exca-
vation hole, wrenching my knee out of its joint.

Mom came to the hospital, took a look at my kneecap, which
resembled a knot in a piece of wood, and looked as though she
might get ill herself.

"I got our all-star baseball game this afternoon," I said to her.
"Am I going to get out of here in time?"

Once again, because of my injury, a doctor solemnly informed
her that I would never play sports. While I was growing up, that
seemed to be the opinion of the whole medical establishment.

The women in my family have always been strong. My mother's
father, Army Major Willie T. Brickhouse Jr., perished in the
Vietnam War in 1967, when she was fifteen years old. My grand-
mother, my mother's mother Mary, raised four daughters. One of
them, my aunt Karen Weeks, was murdered in South Dakota when
I was ten years old. Mary stepped in and raised Karen's three sons,
her grandsons.

One of those grandsons, Kody Weeks, was originally a problem
child, very difficult, with a restless disrespect for adults. Eventually
Kody proved too much for even Mary to handle. Then my mother
stepped in and helped raise him.

Ronde and I had just left for college, but instead of kicking back
and pursuing all the personal goals she had set aside in order to
raise us, she went through the whole adolescent boy experience for
a second time.

The Geraldine Barber school of parenting succeeded once again
in her nephew's case. Kody thrived under my mother's care. He
eventually entered the U.S. Air Force and served in Iraq. His life is
what it is today because of my mom. She employed the same brand

of disciplined parenting with Kody that made my brother and me solid citizens who are respectful to others. My mom doesn't take any back talk. Geraldine may be the nicest lady in the world, but if you cross her, she will whup your ass.

There were times during my childhood when the pressure showed, not on her, but on us. She sometimes spent all day at an office and then took in transcription work at night. I remember evenings when my mother would feed us dinner, carefully oversee our homework, and then tuck us into bed. I'd hear the door open and close as she left for her third job of the day. We would lie there and cry out of sheer loneliness.

Even with Ronde right there in the room with me, I felt something akin to despair, like the darkness was going to come and swallow me up, taking me away from my brother and my mother. In general, I was a happy, carefree kid. But sometimes at night I would become inconsolable and lost.

We were alone because our father, James "J.B." Barber, left us when we were four years old. I don't have any early memories of having a dad at home. Again, Geraldine was such a powerful role model and force in our lives that in a sense Ronde and I didn't miss him. We were a family of three. Our circle was complete.

What did I feel for my father? Not love or hate. Those emotions are too strong. It was something worse. Indifference.

But in another sense, I realize that I still have hang-ups about not growing up with a dad. Maybe my life has been like that of other abandoned sons: a long search for a father figure. I know that at different times coaches, teachers, and other adult males have served that function for me.

Bob Tisch was a father figure, and so was Wellington Mara. It's a culturally loaded dynamic, I know, for an African-American man to become the protégé of older patrician males who identify themselves as "owners." But perhaps the reality of it is more complicated than knee-jerk politics can explain.

The year I was born, the father-I-never-knew played football. He was just coming off a celebrated college career as an All-American running back at Virginia Tech. He never played in the NFL, but he did attempt to play professionally, in a rival outfit that called itself the World Football League (WFL).

The WFL lasted only from 1974 to 1975. J.B. signed up alongside NFL veterans such as Ken Stabler, Paul Warfield, and Larry Csonka. From the very first, the enterprise was financially shaky. In Portland, fans pitched in with potluck to feed the players. In Charlotte, the Hornets once had their uniforms confiscated when they didn't pay their laundry bills.

So the WFL went belly-up. J.B. was cut before he ever played in a game. Maybe bottoming out in pro ball led J.B. to bottom out in his life. He left us three years after his football career was over. Later on, he turned his life around through a Christian ministry. He's now a doctor of divinity.

I rarely saw my father when I was growing up. In our early adolescence, Ronde and I were at a wrestling meet at our Hidden Valley Junior High when J.B. surprised us by showing up.

Wrestling was something we started only because we got cut from the basketball team. Ronde and I wound up loving the sport, and each of us won district championships. I wrestled in the 134-pound weight class. We were identical, but we didn't want to compete directly against each other. Ronde lost eight pounds and wrestled in the 126-pound class.

I don't know how J.B. knew we would be in a match that afternoon, but there he was. I remember him walking over to Ronde and me. I felt a whole platoon of conflicting emotions battling it out for supremacy.

"Hey," my father said. "Tiki, Ronde?"

I watched his eyes, and I realized something. *He doesn't know which of us is which.* That crystallized the situation for me right there: his not knowing which of his identical twin sons he was talking to. Being so out of it, being so removed from the day-to-day, get-up-and-fix-breakfast reality of his children's life.

My gut churned. Hurt, pride, longing, fear, indifference, confusion, and anger, lots of anger—everything mixed up inside me. My face showed only a single reaction: coldness. My expression was a mask. I glanced over at my brother. No smile, no emotion either.

"What are you doing here?" I asked. "Who are you really?" Did I ask that last question out loud? I can't remember. But that was the heart of it for me, the hidden, unanswerable question that dogged me on the relatively rare occasions when the thought of my father came up.

Who are you really?

Can you be my real father? You left me before memory, when I was three years old. Who are you? Just some guy. A last name. A genetic donor. A cloud shadow passing across the bright sunshine of my brother and my mom, my real family. What gives you the right to show up at my wrestling match?

Who are you really?

For a long time, I didn't realize that it was a question I was actually asking of myself.

Anyone who has grown up in a small town knows the claustro-phobic feel and the sense of isolation you can get. A spontaneous afternoon adventure with Ronde when I was in my early teens had the unintended side effect of expanding my horizons quite literally beyond Roanoke.

A lazy summer day—but Ronde and I were too restless to be lazy. We were on our bikes, as usual, but had already ridden through our neighborhood, our park, all our usual haunts.

I think it was Ronde who first suggested it.

"Let's go knock on Debbie Reynolds's door, see if she answers."

Debbie Reynolds—the movie star, song-and-dance entertainer, Hollywood fixture—had married a Roanoke real estate developer named Richard Hamlett and moved to a house in the hills above the city.

I didn't really know who Debbie Reynolds was. Ronde didn't either. We had never seen *Singin' in the Rain*. I had no awareness of the big Eddie Fisher/Liz Taylor/Debbie Reynolds love triangle, which was the biggest Hollywood scandal of the 1950s.

But we did know that Debbie Reynolds was the mother of "Princess Leia," a.k.a. Carrie Fisher. And that was enough for us. Even though we were only two years old when it came out, *Star Wars* was a constant obsession for Ronde and me from very early on. We felt the pull even though Debbie Reynolds was, at best, *Star Wars* once removed.

So we headed out. Across the Roanoke beltway highway, then under construction. Out of the Roanoke valley and into the hills. In the full heat of a Virginia summer, it was a hard, leg-pumping ride. Back then I didn't know what a cardiovascular workout was, but this was a real lung-burner.

If we hadn't had each other, I think we would have given up. That's the way it was with Ronde and me. Neither one of us would say "I quit," no matter how much every cell of our bodies was screaming it. My childhood with my twin was a contest to the finish—and it isn't over yet.

A bike ride of four or five miles, straight up. When we finally got to the house, we found it big enough and impressive enough for the mother of a princess.

"Go ahead and knock," I said.

"You go."

"No, you."

After a little back and forth like that, we decided to go up to the door together. I wasn't going to pedal all that way and not take a shot.

But she wasn't home. No one was. I wonder how we would have appeared to her, two ragtag brothers, sweaty and breathing hard. What did we think were we going to do, ask for her autograph?

"You know the good thing about coming up here?" Ronde said. "It's all downhill going down."

When we turned back from the door, though, we both stopped in our tracks. Spread below us was our hometown, but the view didn't stop there. It kept widening out, over the green Virginia countryside, to Brush Mountain and the Alleghenies to the west.

"Whoa," said Ronde. "So this is how rich people live."

That wasn't quite what the moment meant for me. I don't think I fully grasped it at the time. The view was beautiful enough, sure, but what really impressed me was the perspective it gave to my life. I saw my Roanoke world as small and contained, dwarfed by distance.

There's a big world out there.

That was my private thought, one that I carried with me as my brother and I careened down the roads, wind whistling, screaming our lungs out, effortlessly coasting for miles.

I don't want to place too much meaning on it, but everyone has moments in their lives when they wake up. And turning around to see that view was one of mine. Just a first tantalizing vision of opportunity, of the world that lay beyond the borders of my childhood. I returned to that view in my mind again and again without quite knowing why. I just knew that I wanted to get out and see the world beyond Roanoke.

My mother embraced the ideals of the civil rights movement, wholeheartedly following Martin Luther King's principle of determining a person's worth by the quality of his character. She worked hard to expose us to as many different cultures as she could. She brought books into the household and opened our world through reading.

Ronde and I attended Cave Spring High School, which back then had a student body that was about 95 percent white. I never felt discriminated against or threatened in any way. In fact, my brother and I fit smoothly into the social fabric of the school. I had a girlfriend who was part of that 95 percent all through my teenage years. It was no big deal.

Up until high school, Ronde and I dressed the same way and spent almost all of our time with each other. I was painfully shy. I didn't know how to converse with people I didn't know. All through high school, when most of our peers were busily sorting out issues of identity, Ronde and I didn't venture very far out of our shells. We remained self-contained. He was more extroverted than I was, but still, we relied on our shared twin identity.

The people who knew us could tell us apart easily, just from our different personalities. Other people might have had difficulty, but as I said, we didn't venture that far out of our cocoons to find out. We weren't show-offs and we didn't have the confidence to pull any of the switcheroo tricks commonplace with identical twins. In fact, we did it only once while we were at Cave Spring, during a homecoming parade.

Ronde was injured and not playing. My coach didn't want me, as an active player heading into a game that night, to march. So Ronde dressed up in Cave Spring Knight body armor and rode in the parade as me. Outsiders always imagine that our lives might be a constant game of mistaken identities, like in some Shakespeare play, but it wasn't that way at all. We were more *Family Matters* and *Growing Pains* than Shakespeare.

When we weren't at home, we were out with our girlfriends. We were lucky because my girlfriend's parents were pretty relaxed people. I could stay at her house all day long. Ronde would come over with his girlfriend, another friend would come over with his, and we'd spend the afternoon watching movies or talking.

On the surface, my situation growing up sounds as though it could be a prescription for trouble. A single mom, working so hard that she's often out of the home, with two adolescent boys granted a huge degree of independence.

But it was an innocent time. I didn't party. Athletics took up a lot of my after-school hours.

I had football. My mom had definite ideas about young people playing such a rough contact sport (maybe she still had those doctors' warnings ringing in her ears), so it wasn't until we reached our teens that Ronde and I did any serious playing. And it wasn't until I played on the Cave Spring Knights in high school that I fell in love with the game.

Believe me, I know all the criticisms hurled at the game of football, and I even agree with some of them. Critics say it's a bloated, dominant culture that glorifies violence. Fans of baseball see it as a stop-and-start, back-and-forth game. And others can't understand the appeal of a bunch of muscle-head males bumping into one another and falling down.

Yes, yes, yes. I know all that. As a culture, perhaps America takes the game too seriously. But it's a basic, elemental universe, one of the last remaining zones where violence and domination sort out who is top dog. That's football's glory, and its curse.

The game of football doesn't transfer well to the real world. You can't treat your friends, neighbors, or loved ones the way you treat your opponent on the football field. If you did, you'd be rightly arrested and hauled off to jail. I know many NFL players who have difficulty making that distinction between proper behavior on the field and off of it.

So while we normally should keep the beast within chained up, the football field is where we unleash it. How great is that?

For a sixteen-year-old boy in a Virginia high school in the early 1990s, football was pretty much the coolest thing that ever happened. I didn't do drugs. Football was my rush. Or, more specifically, rushing was my rush.

I remember the Friday night I fell in love with football. Just recently my mother brought some videotapes out of storage, footage from a Knights game in my junior year of high school.

Watching the jerky, fifteen-year-old black-and-white images sucked me back to the moment like a time machine.

An off-tackle run to the right. We wore black jerseys, with high black socks that accentuated the old-fashioned feel of the film. I watched as we broke huddle and lined up in what was then a standard I-formation, me as the tailback behind the quarterback. There was Ronde, split off to the right. It was one of the last seasons we would play on the same side of the ball.

I had just torn off an eight-yard first-down run, so we had a first-and-ten at their forty. Keeping it simple, the coach called a handoff. The quarterback took the hike and placed the ball in my gut.

Seeing the play sixteen years later, I realize that it didn't have a lot of subtlety. I simply took off running. It was all about speed. I angled toward the line of scrimmage and crossed it just as Ronde bounced off a defender, clearing my way. Then I doglegged my angle somewhat, aiming for the right corner, where the goal line and the sideline intersected.

I turned it on. Watching the video, I can still feel the joy of that move. I was gangly, all arms and legs, and I didn't have much heft to me at all. But I had a rate of acceleration that took everyone by surprise. No one could get an angle on me. When they ran to where they thought I would be, I was already gone.

It looks a little comic on tape, like an old Charlie Chaplin movie. How is that one guy moving so much faster than all the other guys? Ronde helped block a couple of defensive backs, but I left him behind too. Then it was just me and the safety. On the video, you see him extending his body at the five yard line, reaching out for me, missing by a couple of feet, then falling on his face.

I crossed the goal line with no one near me.

My happiness wasn't about beating the safety (well, maybe a little). It wasn't about the cheering. It wasn't the screams of my teammates. It was a private feeling I had within myself of pride and accomplishment and victory. A sense of freedom I had never before experienced. A hint of something else, too. *I could be great at this*. I was happy, higher than I'd ever been before, and I had only one thought. *Let's do it again*. That single moment kicked off my decade-and-a-half passion for the game of football.

Parents often come up to me and ask, "How do I do it? How do I make my kids act like you did when you were in school?"

How do you do *The Wonder Years* right? It's simple, but it's hard. The simplicity of it is this: You have to surround yourself with good people. That's the whole prescription, right there. The hard part, though, is how to figure out if someone is a good person.

Ronde and I were lucky. We had each other to feel out those decisions together. If you're by yourself, you're more likely to proceed by habit. "Oh, I'll hang out with him again." Before you know it, you're sucked into something that is detrimental to your life.

Because there were two of us, we had a built-in, automatic reality check. When we were thirteen, around the time of our epic bike ride up to the castle of Princess Leia's mother, I remember proposing to Ronde that we hitchhike from Roanoke down to Blacksburg, where Virginia Tech was located. Just for a lark, just to bust loose, just to get out of our hometown.

"We can't do that," Ronde said. "Can you imagine if we couldn't get back home, what Mama would do?"

"Yeah, you're right," I reluctantly agreed. I don't know what would have happened if we had hitched to Blacksburg. Probably nothing bad. But maybe an encounter with drugs, a fight, or an arrest. If I had gone ahead and made that particular choice, my life today might have been totally different. And there were a lot of choices like that, up and down the line.

Ronde and I had each other as our conscience. For most people, a conscience is an internal thing. For me and my brother it was right there beside us.

If I were going to give a young person advice, it would be to find what I always had in Ronde: a friend who is always truthful with you and who is not afraid to tell you what you need to hear, not just what you want to hear.

I was a borderline geek. I cared about school. My girlfriend, Robin, was the same way. In fact, on some levels, Robin and I felt competitive. We got along, but there was an underlying clash that was always present. We would debate each other. We were in the same English class. She was the liberal tree-hugger feminist, a very intelligent, straitlaced girl, and I was the athlete, a very intelligent minority boy.

Robin was one of those people who kept me on the straight and narrow. I remember once, during Senior Beach Week, when the whole class went to Virginia Beach, I had my one and only under-age experiment with alcohol—a wine cooler. Robin never drank, and she was upset when she heard what I did. She wouldn't talk to me for two hours.

I was a late bloomer, shy and serious. But in my interior life, I had a finely calibrated sense of how other people reacted to me.

"You're such a good athlete," one of my teachers said, soon

after I entered Cave Spring High. And it was true. I'd go on to be All-District and All-Region, gaining 3,680 yards and forty-one touchdowns on 567 carries in football, and lettering three times in track. I was male athlete of the year a couple of times. So was Ronde.

Over the course of high school, though, I started hearing that "good athlete" tagline a little too often. It began to make me think. *What does that label really mean? Does it mean I'm an athlete rather than a scholar? Does it mean that I'm a "natural" on the playing field, so I don't have to work hard? Because I know I work my tail off.*

The tag started to bother me. Not to a great degree. It didn't keep me up at night. But it began to seem like a double-edged sword. I started to hear a slight challenge in the phrase.

"Oh, you're *only* a good athlete."

Really? Is that all I am?

I am Geraldine Barber's son and Ronde Barber's brother. I eat challenges for breakfast.

So I swore to myself that I would show them. You say I'm just a good athlete and that's all? How about I get straight As? Will you say I'm a good student as well?

Pigeonholes, I decided early on, are for pigeons.

I pretty much got straight As in high school and wound up with a 4.0 average. I went out for the Olympics of the Mind (now called "Odyssey of the Mind"), an academic competition that emphasizes creative problem solving. At graduation, I was school valedictorian.

I was a nerd in high school, a nerd who was a star running back, but a nerd nonetheless. Only that single time did I ever take a drink, and otherwise I never put a beer or a wine cooler or anything alcoholic into my body. I never smoked, tobacco or otherwise. I walked the Geraldine Barber path.

I didn't feel much peer pressure, probably because Ronde was the only real peer in my life. I didn't really need any friend other than my brother. He felt the same way. That self-contained attitude helped give us some sort of mystique with other people, so it turned out we had a *lot* of friends.

As clean-cut as I was, looking back I consider myself a serious rebel. I rebelled against the expectations of others. Against stereotypes. Living on my own terms, judging myself by my own standards—that was my primary takeaway from growing up in Roanoke, and it has served me all my adult life.

Don't put me in a box. Don't do it, because I will make it my goal to bust out of that box. Then I'll dismantle it, put it back together as a soapbox, climb on top of it, and tell you that you're wrong to put people in boxes.

Don't put a label on me, because I will show you another side of myself that won't fit that label. Don't categorize, circumscribe, or limit me. Don't put a check mark next to my name as though you've got me all figured out and you don't have to think about me anymore. Don't say, "He's over here," because then I'll show up over there and you won't see me. Don't nail me down, because I have become adept at prying myself up. Don't type me.

It's not being contrary. It's just a recognition of reality. Walt Whitman said, "I contain multitudes." I think we all do. And when people say to me (as they've said to me my whole life), "You're a great athlete," my response is to thank them politely, but inside I'm replying, "I'm also a reader, a thinker, a father, a husband, an African

American, a newscaster, a twin, a friend, an author, a New Yorker . . ."

That list doesn't end. To infinity and beyond, as Buzz Lightyear would say. Because as soon as you put a period at the end of the sentence describing who you are, they might as well fit you with what a friend of mine used to call "the old wooden kimono" (a coffin): You're dead.

Actually, the problem isn't so much when other people pigeon-hole you. You can always sidestep that, or ignore them, or fight them. The real problem is when you pigeonhole yourself. That is the worst form of limitation. *I'm just a football player. I'm just a country boy. I don't belong in the great big world.*

We all have our demons, those inner voices that tell us who we are. Some of the time, those voices work to limit us.

I'm an immigrant. I don't have a proper education. I come from a poor background. I'm not as attractive as the people I see on TV. I don't speak well. I'm shy.

Those are the voices of self-fulfilling prophecy.

Race is the worst, most restrictive pigeonhole of all. And the worst legacy of racism is not the clichéd bigot. It's the internalized racism we take into ourselves. The bigoted voice within us, telling us we can't do it because of our skin color, our religion, our background.

Pardon the language, but fuck that.

With the help of my mother and my brother, I busted out of that box in the rural South of the 1980s and 90s, and I am still busting out of it today.

Ronde and I were heavily recruited out of high school by colleges all over the country. A voice on the telephone would say, "Hey, this is a recruiter from UCLA, and I'm on the line with an assistant coach with our football program. Can we talk to Tiki or Ronde?"

At first, when a call like that came in, we were thrilled.

"This is cool," I recall saying to my brother. "These people want us so bad they're actually going to fly us out to their school."

The first half-dozen contacts were great. An ego boost. A hint that the outside world had heard about two brothers in rural Virginia. We weren't nobodies.

But the hectic college recruiting process turned very old, very fast. A phone call a night, then two or three, then they started to come in batches. Ronde and I would wrap pillows around our ears just to shut them out.

"Mom, tell them we're not here!" we'd yell. It's nice to be wanted. But it's also very nice to be an ordinary, anonymous high school senior. There were times when we didn't want the wider world intruding on our lives.

Ronde and I pretty quickly narrowed down our choices to four schools: Virginia, Clemson, Michigan, and—just for a change of pace—UCLA. In retrospect, the whole process was screamingly arbitrary. We were babes in the woods. We just did what felt right.

Michigan had a good engineering program, and that's what I thought I wanted to do, so Michigan made the short list. Clemson boasted a good all-around sports program. Track and field always attracted me. I wanted to be an Olympian, and perhaps Clemson would help me do that. UCLA was an option in case we wanted a radically different lifestyle than the one we were used to.

As the best academic university in the state, UVA automatically went to the top of the list. Not Virginia Tech, because that's where our parents had gone. We didn't want to follow in our father's footsteps. Plus Virginia Tech was only forty miles from where we grew up, just down Interstate 81 in Blacksburg. We wanted to stay close, but not too close.

UCLA fell by the wayside early on. It seemed to us to be on the other side of the world. We'd flown in a plane once in our lives. The Clemson campus, oddly enough, struck us as too athletic. I remember touring the facilities, the gyms, the private dining rooms for football players.

I turned to Ronde and said, "Athletes run this joint."

And that wasn't praise. We were turned off by it. All the gleaming, modern athletic facilities didn't impress us. That wasn't who we were. Right at that point in our lives, we wanted to see substance.

This whole period was an example of the intuitive relationship I have with my brother. We didn't need to talk about choosing schools too much. We just knew. We also knew we'd both go to the same college. Splitting up wasn't going to happen.

We were lucky because we were both very good athletes. That turned out to be a boon for the recruiters. I envisioned them rubbing their hands together, saying, "All we have to do is convince one and we get both!"

We scheduled a visit to Michigan. I was a little skeptical, because the Wolverines' football program is so huge. We knew that the coaches there would probably convert us to positions we didn't want to play. They would probably want me to be a defensive back. While the recruiter didn't come right out and say it over the phone, I heard the same old message between the lines: "You're too small to be a running back."

I've heard that judgment throughout my football life. By the end of high school I had topped out at the height I am today, a fraction over five-nine (I was listed officially in the NFL as five-ten). I wasn't bulked up, and maybe my coaches and scouts had good reason to tell me I was just too little to play my position.

"You're too small."

At times the coaches would vary the actual words a bit. "You'd be really good playing on special teams, returning kicks." Translation: "You're too small."

But reason or logic didn't matter. I always took the words as a challenge. I didn't want to compete against my brother as a defensive back at Michigan. I wanted to run the football.

Before we went to Ann Arbor, the Michigan recruiter was scheduled to come visit us, but he got snowed in and couldn't fly out of Detroit. The weather told us all we needed to know. We canceled our Michigan visit and started to rethink the process.

You've got to remember, at this point each of us was a good athlete, but neither Ronde nor I dreamed of being an NFL star. That goal seemed too far off, too pie-in-the-sky. The University of Virginia was perfect. The school featured a nice balance between academics and athletics. A UVA education would be something that would carry us through our whole lives.

We visited the campus. There was a ton of diversity. I liked the aura of history about the campus, a quality that came across most in the architecture. We spoke with UVA students and alums.

One person we spoke with was Tom Burns, the star linebacker on the Cavaliers and a guy who was literally a genius. Burns "stopped out" in his senior year because he was in the nuclear engineering program with a 4.0 GPA. He had so many research grants offered to him that completing college didn't make sense right then.

People were lining up to pay $50,000 a year for Burns to do pure research. He was once the starting linebacker on the UVA football team and now works for the Defense Nuclear Facilities Safety Board at Los Alamos.

Back then, I was a wet-behind-the-ears high school senior. When I met Tom Burns, I had an immediate reaction: *I want to be that guy*. And with that realization came a corollary: I *don't* want to be the other guy, the one who goes to Clemson and is driving a Mercedes when he's twenty just because he's a football player.

Ronde and I looked at each other.

"You know what?" I said. "We're done with this shit."

"Let's go to Virginia," Ronde said.

We halted the whole process, stopped taking calls from other recruiters. We told our University of Virginia representative, Danny Wilmer, that we were ready to commit. It eventually turned out that I qualified for an academic scholarship to UVA too, but I had to give that up to take the full-ride football scholarship.

On National Signing Day, in February, the colleges make a huge, crazy spectacle out of the recruiting process. Nowadays it's a televised event in some markets. Athletes formally sign letters of intent, with photo flashes going off in their faces and microphones picking up their every word. You'd think it was a meeting of diplomats from the Middle East. It's not. It's just football.

Ronde and I avoided all that. We committed in November, two months early, because we knew UVA was right for us. It let us finish our senior year of high school in relative peace.

TIKI INTERVIEWS TIKI

Q Would you consider reconciling with your father?

A That's a personal issue that seems to be more important to other people than it is to my brother and me. My family is everything to me, and I know which people it consists of and who is outside the circle. Can I see myself speaking to J.B. again, including him in that circle? Never say never. When my father tried to come back into our lives in the late 1990s, my brother and I believed it might be for ulterior motives, since we had both just been drafted into the NFL. As I said previously in this book, what I feel for my father is not love or hate, but indifference. In a way, that indifference scares me more than anything. To feel nothing for your father—that's a heavy-duty weight to carry. But most days, I don't notice it.

THE CAVALIERS

I was always the reserved, straitlaced, intellectual brother. Ronde was always more outgoing; he was a fraction of an inch taller, and much more socially involved. I would have to pull him in to make him work, and he would have to drag me out to make me have fun. Which he did with a vengeance during our first years in college. It's not that we were making up for lost time, but we didn't hold back, either.

Robin and I had broken up right before we left for college. She went to UVA also, and lived in a dorm right across from me. We would see each other all the time. But it was as though she had turned into a different person. Then again, everybody does that in college, if they're open to new experiences.

I was a new person too. Every weekend for a couple of years at UVA, Ronde and I would go down to Rugby Road, where all the frat houses were lined up, and drink beer and party. At the end of the night, we'd wind up staggering two miles back to our dorm room. It was stupid, but that's what we did.

Around campus, football players were not a big deal. By and large, no one cared. UVA wasn't a powerhouse football school like Florida State, Ohio State, or Auburn. The UVA sports program was more second tier—it was serious, a major college program, but not all-consuming. Football at UVA was just part of the mix. Football players were, for the most part, just "That Guy." A student might say, in passing, "Oh yeah, he's in my economics class." We weren't considered special just because we played the sport.

That's actually what I liked most about UVA. All my life, I've appreciated the benefit of flying under the radar. I started out slow and low-profile with the Cavaliers, the same way I would do four years later with the Giants. Even though as an upperclassman I became a high-profile player, I was never treated like one. So it never went to my head. That under-the-radar experience, in fact, would shape how I eventually approached the NFL.

If I had gone to Clemson, say, on a football scholarship, I would have been treated differently, relative to the average Clemson student. That experience might have shaped me in a much different way than my time at University of Virginia did. They are very impressionable years, the late teens and early twenties. I could have wound up with a totally different outlook on life.

As it was, I thrived. Meeting new people, busting out of my hometown, taking challenging coursework—the whole period was tremendously exciting for me. I started at the engineering school but soon transferred to the McIntire School of Commerce. I loved computers and computer programming, the puzzle-solving part of writing code. I envisioned a career in information technology or communications. In a way, I wasn't that far off.

As John Lennon once said, "Life is what happens to you when you're making other plans." Right in the middle of my University of Virginia experience, at the end of sophomore year, I met the love of my life, Virginia Joy Cha.

Ginny.

As part of my commerce degree I was required to take an introductory computer science class, CS-120. Ginny's major was sociology in business and industry, and she took CS-120 as an elective. I noticed her right away, but it was the end of the semester, in the spring of 1995, before we started talking.

It wasn't romantic at the start. It was friendship. My other dorm roommate, James, was also in the class, and he became smitten with Ginny's roommate. He asked her out, but Ginny's roommate didn't want to go on a date alone with a guy she didn't know. So we all went: Ginny, her roommate, James, Ronde, and I. To Outback Steakhouse, which represented the finest in affordable dining in Charlottesville.

Ginny was dating someone at the time, as was I, so that took some of the pressure off to hook up right away. It allowed us to be natural with each other. And one thing I reacted to from the start was how quick this woman was. I felt challenged by her, intellectually, emotionally, socially.

We went our separate ways over the summer of 1995 and didn't really start seeing each other seriously until the next fall.

"Why didn't you call me?" I asked her when we met on Grounds, as the UVA campus is called.

"Why didn't you call me?" Ginny answered.

"Because you had a boyfriend!"

That might have been a little too scrupulous for her taste, but we started dating that fall and stayed together after that. I didn't really get to know her parents until Ginny had to have an emergency appendectomy that year. Her father was very guarded, but I think I won him over when he saw that I had assembled all my books and stayed overnight in the waiting room, doing my classwork, until I was sure Ginny was out of danger.

"I think he's okay," her father said to her mom.

Ginny's background fascinated me. On the one hand, her family represented everything I fantasized the traditional American family to be. Her father, Won Cha, worked as an electrical engineer, while her mother, Nga, stayed home and took care of Ginny and her sister. Even though it is no longer anywhere near the norm, that Ozzie-and-Harriet lifestyle still holds sway, especially for a boy who grew up with a mother balancing three jobs.

On the other hand, Won and Nga Cha had an incredible story, one that would put the white-picket-fence Ozzie Nelson family in perspective. Won was born in North Korea, was educated in Japan, and eventually had to swim a river between North and South Korea in the dead of night to start a new life. He worked as an engineer for the U.S. government in Vietnam, where he met his wife. In 1975, they escaped *Miss Saigon*–style, days before the North Vietnamese army took over. They emigrated to the Washington, D.C., area and named their newborn second daughter after her birthplace, the great state of Virginia.

I found Ginny incredibly easy to talk to, but I knew we were from different worlds when Ginny casually mentioned her high school's planetarium.

"You had a *what* in high school?" She didn't think it was any big deal. Later on, when we visited Hayfield High in Alexandria together, I saw not an ordinary high school but a whole campus, sprawling, beautifully maintained, with amenities like a rubberized running track, professional-grade baseball diamond, and, yes, a planetarium. For the prom, she had felt it only natural to rent a limo.

"What are you talking about?" I said. I am not sure a limo service even existed in Roanoke when I was in high school.

But Ginny was there before I broke out as a Cavaliers running back. She knew me before I had stats. I liked that when we first met and fell in love, I was everyday, ordinary Tiki to her, not a star athlete. That business was all to come.

One reason I loved my experience at UVA was that I loved the football program there, primarily because the head coach at that time was the great George Welsh, and my running-back coach was the excellent Ken Mack.

Welsh, especially, was more than a coach to me. He was another one of my father figures, an inspiring former navy man who acted as a true mentor. To a large degree, George Welsh taught me how to be a man, how to face responsibility, how to step up, even how to shave, which has served my razor-happy chrome dome well over the years.

I played for the Cavaliers my first year, but not a lot—just a couple of touches. Ronde red-shirted, meaning he practiced with the team but did not play. His limited participation in the program would not count against his four-year NCAA college eligibility. We found ourselves in a strange twilight zone. I was playing major college football in a very minor way, and Ronde was not doing anything at all. He was sitting on the bench. Not exactly an auspicious beginning.

During my second year, I played the same minor role. I got more carries, maybe twenty total all year long. Meanwhile, Ronde broke out. He had played safety in high school, but at Virginia they moved him to cornerback. His second year at UVA—officially his first year of eligibility—Ronde had ten interceptions, second in the country. He was named Atlantic Coast Conference (ACC) rookie of the year. Ronde became a star.

Not me. I was just a guy doing kickoffs and punts. My running-back coach, Ken Mack, told me that if I wanted a larger role on offense, I'd have to get bigger and tougher.

I saw the road fork in front of me right there.

It was 1995, the spring of the '95 season, around the time I met Ginny. That previous year, in track and field, I had tied a school record in the long jump. My choice was to stay the weight I was, 175, and keep my speed. I was very fast. The measure of speed for football players is the forty-yard dash. When I weighed 175 pounds, I ran the forty in 4.28, which is smoking fast and is still the team record.

Getting bigger meant that my track-and-field Olympian dreams would fall by the wayside, because although Ronde and I ran relay, my best event was the long jump. Carrying twenty extra pounds, I knew I wouldn't be jumping for twenty-five feet anymore.

So that spring, Ken Mack laid it out for me: Stay at 175 and be a sprinter/long jumper, or bulk up to 200 pounds and be a football player. The choice was put to me in just so many words. Either get bigger and stronger or you'll remain relegated to a peripheral role with the Cavalier offense.

I chose to get bigger and stronger. In my effort to bulk up, I started taking creatine, an organic, legal, and fairly common performance enhancer, which nonetheless proved detrimental to my overall athletic health.

Creatine draws water into your muscles. It lets your muscles get fuller when you're working out, which makes them stronger. But when the fluid then flushes out of your muscles during exertion, you tend to cramp and pull.

I still ran track just to stay in shape and keep my speed, but I stopped competing after my junior year. I got big. In fact, I got bigger than my frame could handle. As a result of taking creatine, I started pulling hamstrings like crazy. I'd get hurt all the time running sprints. That was frustrating, but the whole training regimen eventually accomplished my ultimate goal.

When the fall 1995 football season rolled around, just a few months after Ken Mack sat me down and we had our talk, I had put on fifteen pounds. Because I was bigger, because I worked out and applied myself, I was ready when an opportunity opened up. The starter in front of me got injured—pulling a hamstring, ironically enough. Suddenly I was UVA's first-string running back.

August 27, 1995. Sunday night, the Pigskin Classic—the nationally televised game that traditionally opens the college football season. The University of Virginia Cavaliers against the University of Michigan Wolverines. The matchup was almost unprecedented, since ACC schools normally wouldn't play against a Big Ten team except in a bowl game. I had played in televised games before, but not in front of such a huge audience. In a very real sense, this game represented my debut on the national stage.

It's the oldest cliché in football: Big players make big plays in big games.

I've accomplished big plays in big games throughout my college and pro career. To be able to do it requires a little bit of cockiness and a little bit of ego. A certain kind of arrogance is necessary to play the game at its highest level. You have to be good and know it. If you don't know it, then you're not going to be successful.

You can't be afraid to fail. The football field is even more unforgiving than life. As soon as you start entertaining thoughts of failure, you're going to fail. So I never doubt myself. Failure never enters my mind. Even when I'm in a situation fraught with failure, my inner voice is always positive. Third down and twenty? No problem. I will be successful.

For the Pigskin Classic that year, my teammates and I got on the plane to travel to Ann Arbor, and right away I realized there was something wrong. My head hurt horribly. A needlelike pain burned in my ear canal, to the point where I was almost crying.

As soon as we landed, I called my friend Beth, who was the Cavaliers equipment manager. "I'm dying," I moaned. "I need help."

Beth went into overdrive. She called the team doctor, who set me up with an IV and antibiotics. I tried to sleep, but I spent the most restless night of my life. This would be my first college start ever. I hardly slept at all.

I got up the next day and felt good. Not just good, but fantastic. We went out against Michigan and the Cavaliers played a terrific game. I was able to run the ball. Nobody thought we belonged in the same stadium with the Wolverines, but this team, the Cavaliers of my junior year, surprised everyone in the country.

Ronde intercepted a pass to set up a scoring drive. At the start of the second half, it was my turn. We were backed up a little bit and it was third down. George Welsh sent in a draw. I took the handoff from quarterback Mike Groh and got nailed almost before the play could develop. Jarrett Irons, a massive Wolverines linebacker, just destroyed me, putting a hit on my shoulder that separated it.

Somehow, I didn't go down. I bounced to the outside and, my arm throbbing and hanging limp, was off for an eighty-one-yard touchdown run. I couldn't lift my shoulder, but at that point we had the game comfortably in hand. That was my last play. I had to come out of the game because of my shoulder.

With twelve minutes to go, the score was 17–0 in our favor. Dislocation and all, I watched with disbelief from the sidelines as Michigan rallied. They tied it on the last play of the game with a pass to the back of the end zone. Then they kicked the extra point for the win. Final score, 18–17, Wolverines.

A bitter loss, but the game contained the seeds of our best season. Playing a national powerhouse almost to a draw gave us a boost of confidence even in the midst of defeat. After that start, both the Cavaliers and I went on an incredible streak. I rushed for one hundred yards in seven straight games. Two of our three losses (against Michigan and Texas) came on the last play of the game.

We finished up the season against the number one team in the country, the Florida State Seminoles, who were steamrolling that year toward another national championship. The Cavaliers had never beaten them. In fact, Florida State had not lost to an ACC team in the four years since it had joined the conference. The

Seminoles enjoyed pure unadulterated dominance against most of their opponents.

A Thursday night game, again, nationally televised. A Cavaliers home game in a new home—Scot Stadium, with 45,000 fans screaming for us in the pouring rain. But it looked hopeless. Every poll ranked Florida State number one. UVA wasn't ranked at all. What chance did we have?

It was mystical, that game. We arrived at the stadium, and the student sections were already filled three hours before kickoff. Mass delirium. The rain had started earlier in the day and hadn't let up, so the atmosphere under the lights was strange, misty. On the drive in, the roads were a mess, with pools of standing water. But this was a new natural field, with state-of-the-art drainage. We walked out onto it, and the condition of the grass was perfect.

During our first offensive series, I fumbled, and Florida State capitalized quickly. Three minutes into the game, and the Seminoles were up 7–0. A typical Florida State-versus-Virginia mismatch. The Noles are blowing out the Cavs once again, right?

But then, on our next series, we ran an option play. At the college level, teams don't audible a whole lot, because it's too complicated a mechanism, but our playbook had a single checked play. It was designed for use when the defense dropped their safeties down into the box (the rectangle near the line) to stop our running game. That's what all our opponents were trying to do—stop the run. Meaning, stop me.

Third and eight. We were lined up on the thirty yard line. I saw the safety coming down. At the same time I heard Mike Groh stand up and audible the option. The truth was, he wasn't an option quarterback, and I wasn't an option tailback, but there it was. The option would give us the best chance to be successful against the defense that the Seminoles were running.

Groh took the snap, faked a run, and pitched the ball to me. The safety froze in place. I found a crease, blazed through the secondary, and ran for a sixty-four-yard touchdown.

A momentum changer. I could see the light come into the eyes of my teammates. I felt it in my own eyes. Groh screamed, totally pumped, "We can play with this fucking shit! We can beat these guys!"

This was Florida State, a team packed with great athletes, and I had just outrun them all down the sideline for a score.

We believed. The 1995 Florida State–Virginia game is still broadcast today on classic sports channels. Our defense played phenomenally. We survived four turnovers. Will Brice, our punter, kept Florida State pinned back, so the Noles could never get anything going on offense.

When we had the ball, we counteracted the awesome speed of their defenders with more option plays, and with draws, rollouts, and screens. I rushed for 193 yards, had forty-five receiving yards, and scored a second touchdown on a reception. With receptions, rushing, and returns, I had 301 all-purpose yards.

Big players make big plays in big games.

It came down to the end. The score was 33–28. The home crowd was in hysterics. If the score stood, it would be the upset to end all upsets. With a minute-twenty left, Will Brice punted the ball deep, again pinning the Florida State offense back against its goal line.

The Seminoles would have to drive the length of the field. On the other hand, six points would do it. They've got to score a touchdown, but they don't even have to bother kicking the extra point.

The Florida State offense ran a pass, then a successful draw, eventually bulling its way to our six yard line. The Seminoles called a time out with four seconds on the clock. They had time for a single play.

If you absolutely, positively have to stop one play to win, what do you do? Do you anticipate a pass? Florida State was pass-happy and had thrown an incredible sixty-eight times already that night. But that might mean they would go counterintuitive on us and run. We faced Warrick Dunn, one of the best college running backs ever, who would go on to play with Ronde at Tampa Bay and is now a star with Atlanta.

The crowd had already stormed out of the stands once. The officials stopped the game to get everybody off the field. The tension was almost unbearable. On rebroadcasts of the game, the cameras show my teammates and me on the sidelines, holding one another's hands like children. A few of the Virginia fans curled up in a fetal position, watching to see what was going to happen.

Florida State ran a trick play. Instead of their QB, Danny Kanell, accepting the ball, their center made a direct snap to Warrick Dunn. He cut right. He was going in for a sure, game-winning score. It was over.

Except . . . at the last second, just before Dunn would have scored, Adrian Burnim, one of our safeties, met him at the goal line. Burnim didn't try to tackle Dunn. He just jumped him and punched at the ball, stopping the play within a foot of a touchdown. Somehow the referee made the right call.

So we won the game. We beat the number one team in the country. Everybody stormed the field. The most unbelievable feeling I ever had in sports, up to that point, was winning the Florida

State game. It represented what football was all about.

But as I recall the euphoria of it, the incredible high that carries over to this day, a terrible regret balances it out. Because on that day life taught me a lesson I hope I never have to learn again.

In my freshman year, we all lived in dorms. The first floor housed guys, the second floor, girls. I was new, and at first I didn't drink or party. But slowly our self-imposed rules loosened. Ronde and I would go down to Rugby and light our hair on fire, as the flyboys say. I had a second-floor friend in the dorm, a girl named Lou.

Lou and I were very close, not in any kind of physical way, but just as a pure platonic friendship. When I would get crazy drunk, I would knock on her door. She would let me sleep in her room. Lou would take care of me. We were as close as anybody could be for a year and a half.

In the craziness and hysteria of our upset win over Florida State, the entire student body rushed the field to uproot the goalposts. A happy, swarming mass of people. And the first person I saw amid the crowd was my old friend from freshman year, Lou. She came up and grabbed me.

"I love you," she screamed. "You're awesome."

In my euphoria I half registered Lou's presence, but didn't really react to her. I was so anxious to get with my teammates that I essentially blew her off. I went to the locker room.

Two weeks later, Lou died in a freak fire.

When my dorm buddy James told me about it, my mind shot immediately back to the game. I recalled that awkward moment with Lou. *Holy shit, what did I do?*

I closed myself off from the rest of the world and wept real tears over her passing. I kept flashing on images of Lou, hanging out with her, her laughing at my idiotic jokes, her taking care of me. She was self-conscious about her weight. Our friendship was unlikely. Playing sports kept me physically centered and in shape. Her complex feelings about her own physicality probably put her the furthest away from a "hard body" as possible.

We even joked about it. "The football player and the shlumpf," she'd say with a laugh. But just as "football player" didn't define me, her appearance never defined her.

That was what was so liberating about being in college. The old rigid social norms of high school fell by the wayside. I felt free to do whatever I wanted. I didn't have to hang with the cool kids. I could discover coolness in whomever I encountered. Lou was a good-hearted person, and I always tried to be good-hearted, so we connected on that level.

After Lou's death, my sadness mixed with anger and pity toward my own behavior. I was furious with myself. In the midst of playing football and doing track and field I always tried to hold on to some sort of standard of behavior.

Don't let your head get turned. Don't let your ego get inflated. Stay down-to-earth.

It was difficult, with thousands of people cheering for me and dozens of backslappers, autograph seekers, and alumni coming up to shake my hand. Easy to get distracted, easy to believe the hype.

I remember a story they used to tell about Red Smith, the great sportswriter. He was sitting among die-hard Cubs reporters in the press box of Wrigley Field, and he heard the other writers crying and moaning about the team losing another game.

"Take it easy," Red Smith said. "A child did not die."

Right. Keep things real. A win over Florida State, that was a passing triumph. The death of a good-hearted girl with her whole life in front of her was an event of a whole different order.

The euphoria of victory and, within it, sadness. The incident made me appreciate what I do, and at the same time placed it all in perspective. No matter how good I am or how talented I become as a football player, and even in the midst of the kind of collective craziness that the game inspires, I have to hold on to who I am and what's important to me.

There was no way I could have known what would happen to Lou. That's life. I lost myself in the sweep of a big win. Maybe being distracted just at that moment was in some way forgivable. But I resolved afterward to keep myself centered, keep the game in perspective, and, if I could help it, never lose myself in that way again.

In the aftermath of my remorse over losing Lou came another blow. During my third year at college, my mother told us that she had found a lump and had been diagnosed with breast cancer.

I remember hearing it and having my life whirl around me as though gravity had stopped working. Geraldine was our rock. She was the one who showed us our path in life, who nurtured and cared for us, who came to all our games.

When Ronde and I left for college, my mother went back to school for a master's in business administration. One time, she called us up and wanted to compare report cards.

"I got all As," she told us, laughing. "What did you get?"

I thought all that would come to a halt when my mom told me she had cancer. All the smiles and jokes were over. Life as I knew it was over.

But once again Geraldine demonstrated what it meant to be strong. Sure, she had the same bouts of self-pity, denial, and depression that afflict everyone who suffers from the disease. But she pulled herself out of it and went on with her life.

Incredibly, through the whole course of her chemo, she never missed one of our games. In fact, she scheduled her chemotherapy sessions around our schedules, so there wouldn't be any conflicts. Her oncologist told her he'd never seen anything like it.

I went through self-pity, denial, and depression of my own. I imagined a void in my life. Without my mother, I would be a puzzle with a huge piece missing. The equation was always Mom + Ronde + me. Three legs of a stool. Take one away, and the whole thing collapses.

I did the best I could to be there for her and help her through the agonizing cancer therapy. Ronde and I tag-teamed it.

"Hey, mom, you have a session tomorrow," I'd tell her on the phone. "Make sure you get some rest today."

Then Ronde would call. "Oh, Mom," he'd say, "don't be such a wimp. Get up and stay active."

The next time around, I would play bad cop to Ronde's good cop.

My life turned into a robotic dream. Football faded into some sort of wallpaper backdrop to my real existence, which was worrying about and praying for my mother. Our team played lousy and our season collapsed. But it didn't matter. I was too tuned into news about my mother's health.

Geraldine scheduled her mastectomy for a Monday. After a day in the hospital, she'd had enough. She went home.

"I couldn't stand lying there with everybody all around me with tears in their eyes," she said.

The next Saturday, still sore and aching from surgery, she was there in the stands. I couldn't help it. I teared up. In good times, love is easy. But in tough times, love turns into an overwhelming force.

Geraldine survived her cancer. She is strong and healthy today, grandmothering my sons and Ronde's daughters, her wide smile lighting up my world. She's an enthusiastic volunteer for the American Cancer Society. I am forever lucky to have her in my life.

The game of football in America processes players with the efficiency of a slaughterhouse. It's an assembly line: Pop Warner to high school to college to the pros—and good-bye. As our college career ended, both Ronde and I had interest from the NFL. We hadn't planned it that way. It's not as though we had mapped out our lives back in Roanoke, aiming for the pros. But we were both locked in. We were on the football assembly line now, and it looked like the San Francisco 49ers might draft me in the first or second round.

That was ironic, since the 49ers were always Ginny's childhood favorites. She never played team sports. Her game was tennis. Ronde and I used to play her and her roommate in doubles. My brother and I had terrible technique, but we simply muscled the ball past Ginny and her partner.

"Hey, I thought you said you could play tennis," I said to Ginny, teasing her about an ace. "But it turns out you really suck."

"Your form is awful!" she shot back. "You're lucky nobody's watching!"

But Ginny followed pro football avidly. Her father liked the game, and he used to watch both football and boxing on television. He used sports as a stress release from his job. Ginny's sister wasn't interested in spectator sports, but Ginny was. It was a good way for her to get to spend time with her dad.

The night before the draft, Ginny and I went to dinner at a cheap buffet restaurant in Charlottesville called the Golden Corral. We had a heart-to-heart. I already knew I had to have this woman in my life. She was a year behind me in school, and I was about to enter the world of the NFL. I wanted to know how she saw the next few years.

"What if I get drafted tomorrow?" I asked her. "Would you come with me?"

She surprised me by not immediately saying yes.

"I have another year of school," she said calmly. "Wherever you go, I'm still going to be here for a year."

"Okay, but what about after?"

"I'll be working in New York."

A small blow. Ginny was unashamedly ambitious. She wanted to be part of the fashion world, something she had dreamed about since she was a little girl. Her goal was to do public relations for a big fashion house. For that industry, the only place to be in the country is New York.

"So you wouldn't go with me?"

"I don't see myself in Green Bay," she said. The Packers were another possibility for me.

The exchange disheartened me. I knew I had to be part of the NFL if I possibly could. But that meant the football assembly line would inevitably convey me away from the woman I loved.

"What about San Francisco?" I asked her, a little desperate. "I thought your idol was Joe Montana."

But I knew it was hopeless. Family was as important to Ginny as her career. She wouldn't want to be a whole continent away from her parents.

During that dinner, she and I faced uncomfortable questions. Is this a long-distance relationship? Do we break it off now?

The next day, draft day, Ronde and I both felt we wanted to avoid the whole circus. I didn't particularly want to sit around while somebody else determined what I would be doing for the next ten years of my life.

So we headed out to play a few rounds of golf.

Ronde and I had picked up the game just that year, courtesy of our old friend and dorm RA, Chip, who was always encouraging us to play. At that time, we sucked at it. Ronde's become a good golfer, with a five handicap, but I'm too muscle-bound. My back is too tight. I can't get a smooth swing.

A pleasant spring day on the UVA golf course, with the NFL a million miles away. Well, maybe we weren't totally isolated. Cell phones were the size of bricks back then, but Ronde and I were both packing.

I took the whole process as casually as I could. I went to the Combine, the cattle call that the NFL holds every year for potential draftees, and I sat for the Wonderlic, the intelligence test the NFL requires to screen out basket cases. (After ten years around wild and crazy NFL players, my advice to the league is they might need to refine the test.)

I learned later that offensive tackles as a group rank highest on the Wonderlic. Lowest scores? Halfbacks. Probably because we get our brains rattled around so much. I hope I at least managed to goose the average a little.

Atlanta seemed to have some interest in me, so I traveled to see then head coach Dan Reeves. But I had heard all through the draft process, from scouts and in the media, that Green Bay was going to be the one. I was thinking I would either go in the first round or at the beginning of the second. Deep in my die-hard Redskin heart, I wanted to go to Washington. But Norv Turner, the head coach of the Skins at the time, laid it out for me.

"My kids are huge fans of yours," he said. "But I can't draft you, because we have too many running backs." It broke my heart.

We were on the seventeenth green when my call came through. I hadn't been playing well, but at that precise point in time I had just sunk a birdie putt—my only under-par hole of the day. I remember shaking my fist in the air, Tiger Woods–style, and Ronde saying that I shouldn't get too cocky. Then my brick of a cell phone rang. We both burst out laughing. It seemed like fate.

Pat Hanlon, director of PR for the Giants (whose family, oddly enough, knew Ginny's family, but I didn't find that out until later) was calling. "I have Coach Fassel on the line for you."

Who? Jim Fassel had just joined the Giants that year. He had formerly been the offensive coordinator of the Ravens and an assistant coach with the Cardinals, the Broncos, and the Raiders. Before that, he had been John Elway's quarterback coach at Stanford.

But I had no idea who Jim Fassel was. I was at sea, standing out there on the bent-grass green. I didn't even know which team was about to draft me.

Another voice came on the line. "Tiki? Jim Fassel. I just want to tell you I'm a big fan of your play. I'm going to draft you the next pick in the second round."

I was jazzed and excited and over the moon. The NFL! But first I had to find out who in the NFL, exactly, was calling me. Fassel himself never said the magic words. But eventually I got the idea.

The New York Giants.

New York.

My first thought, literally, even while Ronde was still pounding me on the back and hollering, was, *Ginny will love this.* The football assembly line had delivered me up directly into the arms of my girl. My professional and private life meshed perfectly. We could be together in New York after all.

Ginny felt the same way when she heard. "After today, I totally believe that destiny and fate really exist," she said.

After I spoke to Ginny and gave her the news, Ronde and I had something to do, something we had promised ourselves since the NFL first showed interest in us. We sat down with our mother.

"Mom," I said to her, "you can quit your job. Ronde and I are going to take care of you from now on."

In a sense, that was the culmination of a long, hard road that the three of us had traveled together, from hard times and three jobs at once back in Roanoke, up through Cave Spring High and then UVA. All the adversity, all the battles we had faced resolved themselves right there. You could forgive the three of us for getting a little misty-eyed. We had made it.

The problem was that I hated New York City and refused to live there. Even though I would be playing for one of the great franchises in sports, I wanted no part of New York.

TIKI INTERVIEWS TIKI

Q Do you want your sons to play football?

A The short answer is that I want my sons to engage in whatever activities will ignite their enthusiasm, passion, and aspiration. Too often, we send our kids onto the football field at too early an age, when they are physically unprepared for such a demanding contact sport. There are exceptions to every rule, but kids shouldn't play football until age ten or twelve, depending on their maturity. Any earlier and they risk alienating themselves from the game. I'm glad my mother held us back from getting too involved too early on. There are other noncontact sports that can prepare you for football when you've finally developed the physical maturity for it: track and field, for example.

DON'T GET BEAT

If you had asked me when I left college if I would ever live in New York City, the answer would have been a categorical "No!"

Even though I am a confirmed New Yorker now, my first visit to Manhattan degenerated into disaster. I left there swearing I would never return. Ginny's sister lived in New York City, so in January 1997, just before I was drafted by the Giants, we came up to visit her.

We took a Greyhound bus from Washington, D.C., and arrived at the Port Authority Bus Terminal on 42nd Street and Eighth Avenue, on the edge of Times Square, just as the winter's worst blizzard hit. I remember stepping out onto the freezing cold Manhattan street, looking up and down and not being able to see a damn thing because the snow was swirling all over the place.

"This is great," I shouted sarcastically into Ginny's ear. "It's a freaking snowstorm."

It was horrible. Absolute chaos. What few cabbies were out were forced by the storm to drive slowly down the middle of the avenues. The sidewalks were so piled with snow the pedestrians walked in the streets. For four long days we were snowbound, stuck sleeping on the hardwood floor of Ginny's sister's studio apartment. The place was tiny, probably the size of the living room of our apartment now. It wasn't romantic. I was miserable.

We couldn't get out; there was no bus service. My mother finally bought us tickets back home. We took a train that seemed to crawl about five miles an hour back to D.C.

"Ginny," I announced after that episode, "I am never, ever going to New York City again."

Five months later, in the 1997 NFL draft, the New York Giants, with the thirty-sixth overall pick, announced their second-round choice: Tiki Barber.

Ginny didn't share my aversion to New York. She wanted to follow her sister. She loved the energy of the place.

"To hell with it," I said, still burned by the memory of the hardwood floors and the claustrophobic apartment. "I'll live in Jersey."

And I did live in Jersey City for a year. I was alone because Ginny was still in school. I had moved up as soon as I graduated in May.

A strange in-between period. Mini-camps were starting, but training camp didn't begin until later in the summer. I knew that when players finished training camp and they didn't yet have a place to live in the area, suddenly they were in a mad scramble for housing. At times they wound up staying in a motel.

I set myself up so I wouldn't have to worry about where I lived after camp. I rented a huge apartment right on the Hudson, with a spectacular view of downtown Manhattan across the harbor. I wanted Ginny to be comfortable when she visited. I thought maybe the view would satisfy her city hunger. But I literally never went into New York. I hung out in Hoboken.

As 1997 training camp started in Albany that summer, Rodney Hampton, then the Giants' all-time leading rusher, expected to be the starter. Charles Way, another UVA alum, who I had known during my first couple of seasons with the Cavaliers, played fullback.

Tyrone Wheatley, another big back, was in camp also. He had been a first-round draft choice a couple of years before out of Michigan, a high-profile college program, where he was MVP in the 1993 Rose Bowl. Tyrone had three inches of height on me and considerable weight.

I was in the mix, but the fans assembled around the summer-baked grass practice fields of SUNY–Albany were not exactly clamoring for my autograph. I was an unknown quantity, a second-round draft choice out of a second-tier school who was, the accepted wisdom had it, a little small for professional ball.

At that point in time, I didn't really feel as though I had hit the financial jackpot, either. My signing bonus was $705,000. My first-year salary came in at $320,000. Even though, technically, that meant I would earn a million dollars, with taxes and savings the reality was closer to half that.

There were things I wanted to do with my money, like buy my mom a house. That is the time-honored first move for athletes, rap stars, and lottery winners. You've got to buy your mama a house.

So that first contract wasn't the pot of gold at the end of the rainbow. I felt more as though playing in the NFL was a good first step.

I might have raised the bar, increasing the average salary of UVA graduates from the class of 1997. But I didn't have the sense that I was set for life.

Some new players think that way. "Hey, I made it into the National Football League. I'll be sitting in a hammock for the rest of my days." This despite the fact that the average NFL career lasts for two years. I thought I might be able to play three or maybe five years. I would do this football thing for a little while and then get on with my real life.

I learned subsequently from Jim Skipper, my first Giants running-back coach, that it could have gone a different way for me with me and the Giants and the draft.

"Teek, I probably cost you a lot of money," Skipper said. This was three years into my Giants career, when I was well established but had yet to blow up.

"What are you talking about?"

"Jim Fassel wanted to draft you in the first round." For the Giants that season, it would have meant the seventh pick overall.

First-round draft picks always garner more money and more publicity. An overall seventh pick in the NFL draft would have been huge. The difference between the seventh and the thirty-sixth pick probably meant literally millions of dollars.

Coach Fassel later confirmed it. It was Jim's first year as a Giants coach, and he wanted to make a statement by bringing in dynamic players. His wish list included a receiver and a running back. He was ready to take me in the first round. The choice was between me and the great receiver out of the University of Florida, Ike Hilliard.

"I convinced Jim [Fassel] that he could still get you in the second round," Skipper said. "I thought you might still be available for our second pick, but I didn't think Ike would be."

I certainly didn't feel resentment when Jim Skipper told me this. I knew the NFL draft was like a military operation, finely calibrated and researched to within an inch of its life—a finely calibrated and researched crap shoot. Every NFL franchise played its chips differently.

For most of my college career, I kept to my under-the-radar comfort zone, until the Florida State game in my junior year. Even after that, I wasn't a huge name across the country. As I've said, under the radar can be a comfortable place to be. It lessens people's expectations, so they are always pleasantly surprised when you exceed those expectations. It allows you the room and time to grow. In my case, it cost me money. But I think the trade-off was a good one.

The second-round pick, plus all the competition in camp, could have daunted and depressed me. How could I ever beat out a great back like Rodney Hampton? Would I wind up third string, behind Rodney and Tyrone? I could have gauged my chances, thrown up my hands, hung up my cleats, and headed back to Virginia to write computer code for a living.

I didn't do that. Ever since I was a kid, I've thrived on pressure. Is that my genetic makeup? Or my upbringing? All I know is that determination is the coin of the realm, on the playing field and off it. At Albany that year I lowered my shoulders and dug in, swearing I'd have the best camp of anyone. There was nothing I could do about Rodney or Tyrone. The only thing I had control over was my own performance.

I was a stranger in a strange land, without my twin brother beside me for the first time in my life, missing Ginny. But I got lucky. One of the first people I met in New York was a sports reporter named Jay Glazer. Back then he worked for the *New York Post*, and he's gone on to great things as a commentator for Fox Sports.

Football players don't always want to make friends with reporters, because they feel they can't trust them. But Jay has been ultimately loyal to me. If he gleaned some inside information about me and I asked him not to write about it, he never did.

I met Jay Glazer when I was sitting in my locker area at a summer mini-camp during my rookie year. All the other reporters were talking to players more important than I was. I was a second-round nobody. But Jay came up to me, and we had a great conversation.

When he left, one of the veterans pulled me aside. "You have to watch out for that dude."

I shrugged my shoulders. "He seemed like a good guy to me."

Jay and I were both young and full of energy. We'd go out. Over the years we've become extremely close. Jay was one of the first non-family members to see both my kids after they were born. When 9/11 happened, he was at my doorstep two hours later. He lost a buddy in the Trade Center attacks. When push comes to shove, you seek out your closest friends, and Jay and I sought out each other.

Midway through camp that rookie year, Rodney Hampton's knee seized up on him. In his mind, I think Rodney already had one foot out the door that season. It appeared he was ready to retire relatively soon, but it's hard for most people to let go. Then his knee caught up with him. He was on the Giants' PUP list ("physically unable to perform") for the foreseeable future.

The landscape shifted. Tyrone and I eyed each other. Nothing overt, but we were both fierce competitors. It helped that I had a different, more mercurial style than he did. Off tackle, where there tended to be more choices, more open seams, I could make things happen. In between tackles, where it was more a question of brute power, Tyrone was the man, or the fullback Charles Way.

Toward the end of the summer during my rookie year, Jim Skipper gave me a heads-up. I had impressed the Giants, he said. "Tiki, you could wind up starting for us here. Keep doing what you're doing."

I had a good camp and an even better preseason. As the regular season opened, I was named the first-string running back for the New York Giants. A reward, and a challenge. Now I would have to prove what I could do.

I started the initial five games of my rookie year, hitting a high note in the first one, the season opener against Philadelphia. I caught a long pass up the sideline and had a couple of good runs. On the ground, twenty attempts for eighty-eight yards, with another thirty yards tacked on catching the ball. My career was promising. I was—beyond all my dreams—starting for the New York Giants.

For five games.

Then, on September 28, 1997, at Giants Stadium, where we were playing the New Orleans Saints, I took a bad cut, got tangled up, and tore the PCL in my right knee.

The PCL. The posterior cruciate ligament. As opposed to the ACL, the anterior cruciate ligament. Common sports injuries have become part of the wider social vocabulary, to the degree that you have people discussing rotator cuffs and separated shoulders over beers at the corner tavern. For a running back, especially for a cutback-style ball carrier like I was, the letters have a ring of doom to them.

PCL.

Doom.

I went down and stayed down. My knee didn't hurt. It just felt odd, as though a body part had been taken from me that I didn't even realize I had. But I just knew. Immediately, subconsciously, I knew that I would never be that same back again—the feinting, dodging, fake-'em-out kind of back that I had been since high school, the kind who misdirects linebackers right out of their cleats.

I was like a trumpet player who had just been told he was going to have to learn the sax. Once you lose a part of you like that, an elemental capability is gone. In the wake of my injury, I became very discouraged. How was I going to play now that I couldn't cut, now that my knee was going to be unstable? I would be nervous every time I tried it out. It was the first time in my life that I felt I was not going to be a good athlete anymore. It was terrifying.

That lyric from the band New Edition kept going through my head. "Aw, baby, is this the end?" My inner dialogue was feverish. *What am I going to do? I might not be able to play this game. I might have a year or two left and then I am going to have to do something else.*

I had seen it happen time and time again. The abbreviation "PCL" or "ACL" floats next to the name of a running back or a wide receiver on the injury report, and their career just fades away like an old soldier. I knew football wasn't forever. I had always envisioned leaving the NFL at some point and moving on with my life. But not yet, and not in this fashion.

But eventually I did come back. I was out for four weeks. I played again at Tennessee on November 9, and by the next month

I was up to twenty-plus carries a game again. But I had lost my starting slot. I was confused about where I was heading. Actually, I knew where my professional football career was heading.

Straight down the tubes.

That first year of pro ball, absence made my heart grow fonder, more tortured, and incredibly lonely. I asked Ginny to marry me. I had to have her in my life.

We were married on May 15, 1999, in the chapel at UVA. The day before, it had poured rain, and more was predicted. Ginny was in tears, since we had planned a big outdoor reception. But the day dawned bright and clear. Everything went off without a hitch, or, in this case, with me getting hitched.

I wore a tux and Ginny a beautiful gown for our afternoon wedding. We had one hundred fifty guests at the Boar's Head Inn, including Geraldine and Ronde, of course, Ginny's family, and many of my old high school friends. As much as I loved her then, the puzzle of where we would land loomed before us.

I knew she wanted to live in the city. It wasn't a battle that I necessarily wanted to fight.

Greater love hath no Virginian, than to move into Manhattan— dirty, cramped, expensive Manhattan—for his wife.

One afternoon during the 1998 off-season, soon after Ginny graduated from UVA, we were driving in the industrial wilds of northern New Jersey, along the Hudson near Giants Stadium. Across the river, Manhattan showed off its glowing, golden towers. It looked like Oz, only without the green.

"Honey," I said, screwing up my courage and making the leap, "let's move into the city."

"Really?" Ginny was pleasurably shocked that I would willingly volunteer to pull up stakes for Manhattan.

But it turned out to be one of the greatest gifts she ever gave me. It took me about two weeks of living in our first apartment, for me to fall in love with the whole vibe of the place. In those two weeks I became a New Yorker. It was a decision that would change my life forever, and I had to be dragged kicking and screaming into it. Sometimes things just happen that way.

One of my main sources of enjoyment living in Manhattan was to watch Ginny take it by storm. She got an entry-level job in public relations. She put in long hours, ridiculous hours. Her working day was exceeding mine by far. She left our apartment at seven thirty a.m. and didn't come back until ten o'clock at night, Monday through Friday. It was crazy.

"You're working yourself into the ground," I told her.

"I like to work," she answered. She was determined to live her dream and didn't want hubby whining about it.

"But I never see you. Maybe we're in a position where you can look for a better-quality-of-life job."

Eventually she did, landing brilliantly exactly where she always wanted to be, doing public relations at a major fashion house, Ermenegildo Zegna. It took me a while to learn how to pronounce the name of my wife's company (it's "zenya" in the Italian pronunciation). Zegna is primarily known for men's fashion, and I had to start dressing a lot better just to keep up with Ginny.

Even though she dealt with media on a daily basis as part of her job, sometimes I regretted bringing sports reporters into our personal life. Ginny was a rock, though. One time a reporter kept dogging her during an interview, trying to tease something out of her about her parents and my relationship with them.

"Isn't there a lot of prejudice against blacks in Korean culture?" the reporter asked.

Ginny was offended at the whole line of questioning but kept her annoyance in check. The reporter would not leave the issue alone. He obviously wanted Ginny to say that Won and Nga Cha were somehow less than happy that their daughter had married an African American.

Finally Ginny was fed up.

"My father lived as a Korean in Japan," Ginny said. "My mother grew up in Vietnam during a real difficult time. Because of their own intercultural marriage, my parents have felt prejudice against them their whole lives. How could they possibly participate in it themselves?"

We've lived in a succession of apartments on the Upper East Side. After a few years, when we thought about having children, we began discussing moving out of New York. Was it really the right place to raise kids?

"Let's go get something to eat and think about it," I said.

So we took the elevator downstairs, walked out of our apartment about two blocks, and had a phenomenal meal of steak frites at a tiny French bistro we went to a lot. While we were eating, the certainty just crept over us. It was almost as though we didn't have to voice our decision, but I did anyway.

"You know what, Ginny? We're never going to leave here."

New York City was exciting and always full of possibilities. My football career, I thought, was faltering before it really began. If I crapped out with the Giants, I decided, I could always find a job in Manhattan, on Wall Street, maybe, or in the media.

At practice and on the sidelines, I let my discouragement show. I moped. There were some games where I never got into the game except for third downs and punt returns.

They used me on third down because I knew all the pass protection, but I wasn't the same player I had been at the beginning of the season. I was disgruntled about it. I wanted to be who I was my first few rookie games. That was the guy I knew from high school and college. That was the guy I had confidence in.

Coach Fassel took me aside. I give him a lot of credit for doing this, because he brought me clarity about what my role was going to be for the Giants. It wasn't the role I would have chosen for myself, but those were the breaks—or, more accurately, the ligament tear.

"Tiki, I like you," Jim began, spooning up the sugar. "You're like my own kid. I'm going to be straight with you now, and I want you to listen. I want you to focus on a different role, because you're not doing good at being the every-down back."

Ouch. Tell it like it is, Coach.

"I want you to concentrate on being the best third-down back and the best punt returner in this league. And then we'll go from there."

Okay. Fair enough. Give me a job, spell it out, and I'll damn sure do it well. That was a legacy of being Geraldine Barber's kid. It started with athletics. Geraldine wouldn't let Ronde and me play sports unless we made good grades. It's part of my personality, to overdo what people ask me to do. So when my mom said I had to do well in school before I could play sports, I didn't just do my homework and show up at school every day. I made straight As.

On the bright side, Coach Fassel was showing faith and confidence in a specific aspect of my game. I started to talk myself into it, using my inner voice to cajole and wheedle some commitment. *You know what? I am not going to let him down.*

So I worked at it. I became a very good punt returner. In 1999 I was second in the league for average yardage. And as a third-down back, I also thrived. I started out with thirty-four catches that first year, 1997, then the next year I had forty-two, and the year after that sixty-six. I was making catches and keeping drives going. The Giants began using me as a return specialist, and that turned my whole game around.

There's no other situation in sports that can match the sheer terror of the punt return. A penalty shot in soccer, or a catcher protecting the plate in baseball, vaguely resemble it, the way a pistol duel might resemble an assault-rifle firefight at midnight. They're really not the same.

Most punts average under four seconds of hang time, plus maybe another second from snap to kick. That means special teams' defenders have the count of five to sprint downfield and terminate your attempt at a runback. But with the rise of specialization in the NFL, it's as if they're manufacturing monster sprinters who can make it to your front door in less than five seconds, just in time to clean your clock.

The punter himself usually hangs back as a last-resort tackler, so there are normally ten of them. My front line is doing its level best to impede their progress. But let's allow the guys who are after me an average weight of, say, 220 pounds. Times ten, that's more than a ton of humanity hurtling in my direction, intent on separating my head from my body.

You can't look at them. All during the time they are tearing ass toward you, you absolutely must keep your eyes on the ball. Your head is tilted back, and your vision is fixed on that damned prolate spheroid tumbling lazily through the air. The ball seems to travel a lot slower than the defenders. You can hear them thundering toward you. Some of them bellow, just to psych you out. Hell, at times I swear I can *smell* them coming down on me.

And I'm standing dead still. Until they're, say, five yards away, coming full speed, I'm a stationary target. It's a test of nerves more than anything else. As the ball arrives and I can finally lower my eyes to see what kind of apocalypse I'm facing, time collapses again. Everything happens in an instant. I morph from a statue into a bolting roadrunner in a fraction of a beat.

My thoughts race. *Twenty guys in front of me. Okay, who's not on my team? How can I evade them? How can I get in the open field?*

You catch the ball, you drop your head, and your first instinct is to fall down and curl up in the fetal position, because a platoon of killers has drawn a bead on you. But what you train yourself to do is this: make a move and see what happens. Take three steps to the right and observe what everybody does. Or three steps to the left. It doesn't matter which way, as long as you don't stand still.

Step right, and see if that screws up the thundering head-separators. See if a hole opens. You only get one cut in a punt return. If a hole opens, you go.

But you have to move, because when you move, you move the defense, too, you move the pursuers, and that's the only way you can get an advantage. Make them commit. They're converging on you, a multirayed vector angling to a point. A football field is 160 feet wide. Ten men occupy, say, sixty or so feet of that space. You've got to find the gaps.

If you don't move, you get trapped, stuck in the cookie jar. But if you take those vital steps to the left or right, all of a sudden the cookie jar lid opens a crack, which means you have a much better chance of getting out of it.

You have to have a real quick step. When you decide where you're going, you have to be there almost as soon as you decide. The easy part is knowing where you want to go. But if you hesitate, if your feet aren't quick enough, you're never going to get there. You're going to get flattened.

You can get hit from any direction. That's the scary part. Sometimes the annihilator comes from behind you.

I returned punts for three seasons, and it helped instill raw nerve in me as a player. I took only one punt back for a touchdown, against Dallas, on *Monday Night Football*, October 18, 1999. ("Big players make big plays . . .") Greg Comella sprung me on that one with a key block. He took a defender and drove him all the way out of bounds. Just dumped him. It was a beautiful thing.

If it works, a punt return can be the most exhilarating play in football. Devin Hester, number 23 from Chicago, is the most explosive kick returner of the current day. I've witnessed him manipulate defenders who are still fifteen feet away from him. He stops them dead, gets them to trip over their own feet. I don't know how he does it.

My other position on the Giants during those years, as a third-down back, was a situational, almost journeyman designation, part of an ongoing trend toward more and more specialization in the NFL. What it meant was that I would come into the game on third and long, and I would pick up the first either on the ground, usually via some sort of draw or play-action, or through the air, on a short pass or a screen. If it was third and seven, I would get eight, if it was third and twelve I would get thirteen. That was the idea, anyway.

In the cold-eyed calculus of professional ball, third-down backs aren't considered tough enough to handle every-down duties, where you are more likely to get knocked around and beat up. But because I had good hands and a quicksilver, cutback running style, I was perfect for the third-down call. So third-down back I was. I didn't quibble. Like the John Fogerty song about baseball, I was more of a "put me in, coach" kind of player. Wherever you tell me to go, I'll go.

I could have tucked my tail between my legs and left the league right at the beginning, after my injury. But that's just not me. The league is littered with running backs who blow out their knees and are never the same again. The game chews them up and spits them out. I have friends who have been that way—their careers end and they say, "Okay, now what do I do for the rest of my life?"

Injuries are always wake-up calls. They remind you, the invincible gridiron warrior, that you're human, flesh and blood, and fallible. Around the time of my injury I began to cast around for options other than football. What I've consistently tried to do all my life is be different. I didn't want to be like some of my former teammates, lost after my pro career ended because I didn't know what I wanted to be when I grow up.

Football is a child's game played by adults. I used to joke around about that with people all the time, wondering what I was going to do when I grew up. And they'd take the question seriously, saying, well, Tiki, you can do this or that or you could do that. I didn't let on that I was, of course, planning carefully for my future.

So it wasn't random that soon after my injury-plagued rookie season, I entered broadcasting for the first time. I just stuck my toe in, taking a radio job, but it represented an entry into a field that would become a passion.

I was thinking about the future, yes, but at the same I was determined to stay in the game, to succeed in the here and now. After I tore my PCL, I wasn't ever going to be the same player. But did that mean I couldn't be successful at football? That was the challenge I was facing, and luckily, a few good people helped me meet it.

The fullback is an endangered species in the NFL. As a kid, my favorite coach was Joe Gibbs of the Washington Redskins. Gibbs was the one who probably put a bullet through the fullback position more than anybody, when he had such great success with the spread offense in the early 1980s.

With the concurrent rise of the West Coast offense, the position of a blocking back just wasn't in the scheme of things. The new offensive systems put three or more receivers wide, stretching out the field side to side, so there wasn't as much need to plow straight into a piled-up middle. Some teams used pulling tight ends to serve what was formerly a fullback's function.

In the NFC, since we tend to be more of a grind-it-out, run-oriented conference than the AFC, there are still a few, proud examples. But whereas before, in the glory years of the Bears' Bronko Nagurski and the Packers' Jim Taylor, teams might carry two fullbacks on their rosters, now it's common to carry one or none at all. It's become, like almost all NFL positions have become, a specialty.

The fullback is like the broom in curling. Clearing the way. The connection between a fullback and a tailback is necessarily a close one, and fullbacks are the teammates with whom I've always been the tightest. I ended my pro career with Jim Finn, whom I always call "Finny," blocking in front of me. But back when I was trying to readjust to my new status as the Giants punt returner and third-down back, my main man, best friend, and power fullback was Greg Comella, fullback par excellence.

The position was in his blood. His father Gene was a fullback, as were his two brothers. The Giants signed him out of Stanford University as an undrafted rookie free agent in 1998. We immediately took a liking to each other. It might sound strange to be saying this about something as basic as football, but we could keep up with each other intellectually, watching film and analyzing defensive sets.

"Hey, Teek," Greg said on the phone to me during the 1999 off-season, after he had already spent a year clearing tacklers out of my way on the playing field. "Want to come train with me?"

Greg was a madman for fitness and strength training. He started in high school. This was his regimen as a seventeen-year-old:

I would always do my lifting before school at six a.m.
It was a ten-week program, three days of lifting per week,
three days of running. Mondays, chest, shoulders, and legs;
Wednesdays, back and shoulders; and the week ended
on Fridays with back, chest, and legs. I also incorporated
auxiliary lifts (deltoids, shrugs, calf muscles) twice
weekly. Each major muscle group included three sets
of between eight and twelve repetitions each.

"I'm going to run this hill out in Ramapo," Greg informed me. I was a Virginia guy. I told him I had never heard of Ramapo. "It's in New Jersey, right off Route 17."

If I had known what I was getting myself into, I might have told Greg thanks, but no thanks. Instead, I took the bait.

"All right, I'll go. What time are you leaving?"

"I get up by five thirty and I'm out of here by six."

"You're kidding me, right?"

"Tiki, c'mon, dude."

I thought of all the times he had smashed 320-pound defensive linemen out of my way. For the kind of services he'd rendered, I felt obligated to at least humor him.

"All right, I'll go with you this one time."

Early the next morning we drove across the George Washington Bridge and threaded through the suburbs.

"Aren't there places you can go to kill yourself that are way closer than this?" I groused, grouchy at that god-awful time of day.

February in northern New Jersey. Near Mahwah, like the Bruce Springsteen song ("Well, they closed down the auto plant in Mahwah late that month"). We got out there to find snow on the ground. Greg's idea of a workout venue was a treacherous two-and-a-half-mile trail in the Ramapo Valley County Reservation. There was no "valley" involved. It was all uphill. It was all ice, all steep, beautiful as a forest but ugly as a climb.

"I think this is a hiking trail," I said to Greg, surveying the route from the parking lot. "For hikers to, you know, like, walk up it." I emphasized the word "walk."

"A lot of people do walk it, no doubt," he replied. "But we're going to run it."

"That's crazy," I said, but he was already off, trotting briskly toward the tree line.

The trail turned and twisted over rocky, icy ground. After 500 yards of it, I was dying.

Greg jogged in place, waiting for me to puff up to him. "You cannot stop running," he stated. "You hear me? No matter what, you can't stop. If you walk, it's too easy."

If I walk, I'll survive.

"C'mon, Teek!"

The hill evolved into the Hill, with a capital *H*. It became the biggest physical challenge that I had ever faced, because I couldn't perfect it. I couldn't master what this Hill was going to give me. But Greg was superb at motivating me.

Greg: "When we get into a game against Keith Bulluck, we need to find his weakness, right?"

Keith Bulluck was a dominating Tennessee Titan linebacker, a worthy adversary who was as mean physically as a snake, and just as quick.

Me: "*Huff, puff . . .*" I'm not even running. I'm barely jogging.

Greg: "Keith Bulluck has a weakness, right? And we can find that weakness, right?"

Me: "*Huff, puff. . .*" *Greg,* I thought, *I can run this hill, or I can answer your questions, but I can't do both at once.*

Greg: "Every human has a weakness, but you know what? This hill? This hill has no weakness. You know exactly what it is going to give you, but you still can't beat it!"

Me: "*Huff, puff* . . . You're right. . . . I'm going to . . . *huff, puff* . . . find a weakness . . . in this . . . goddamn . . . Hill.*"

I never did find one. Over the course of two off-season months that winter, the Hill and I fought each other to a draw. But somehow, the toughness I had to have just to drag my ass up the Hill at six every morning incorporated itself into my mentality as a football player.

Don't get beat. Find a weakness. If there is no weakness, look again. If you can't beat your opponent, at least don't let your opponent beat you. There it was. Greg Comella's philosophy distilled into three words. *Don't get beat.*

It would take us about a half hour to run the Hill. Then we would walk back down in the freezing cold, twenty degrees and blustery, talking. Those talks are how Greg and I became close. We discussed everything, sports and Y2K (remember Y2K?) and the election and Ronde and the future.

More than the physical conditioning that the Hill gave me—much more—was the mental toughness I developed. The Hill didn't give a damn if I ran it or not. It was just *there*. That left the decision totally up to me. Me and Greg. The intensity that Greg has as a person carried over to his intensity as a football player, and as a motivator to me.

So I started to adopt some of these ideals that Greg had. He was gifted as an athlete, but more than that, he was good because of his mind and his character.

On that rutted, muddy trail in Jersey, I began to recognize that I could will myself to be a better player, Greg Comella–style. I would have to start doing some of the same things that he did, start thinking the way he thought. He made me into a follower of details, maniacal about determining weaknesses in our opponents and finding ways to exploit them. The experience changed my view of being a football player.

An added benefit of Greg and me getting to know each other showed on the field. We spent so much time together that he became like a remote-control blocker in front of me. A defensive tackle would be crashing toward me, and I'd be thinking, *I need him to cut this guy RIGHT NOW.* I couldn't scream that out loud, of course, because in the chaos and blitz of football you can't hear anything, and by the time you try to direct someone verbally, it's usually too late.

But sure enough, Greg would cut the guy. Perfectly and at just the right time. Without me saying a thing. It mystified me sometimes. How could he know that? It might have been because we spent so much time together on the Hill, or because we stayed late so much after practice to watch film. Verbal communication became superfluous. We intuited. We developed a Vulcan mind meld.

A lot of time, the message that passed between us was pretty broad. *Don't get beat.*

With that simple philosophy, my performance on the field began to change. I began tearing off positive yardage on almost every carry. I was a third-down back who was performing like a starter. Now all I needed was someone on the Giants coaching staff to notice.

TIKI INTERVIEWS TIKI

Q The Giants have had pretty good talent but haven't performed very well. What's the reason?

A It's all about laying a foundation for winning, and unfortunately as an organization the Giants haven't done that. During my years there, we were the epitome of mediocrity. General Manager Ernie Accorsi had a long reign, and he's a really good man, but in sports you are judged by results. Ernie never demonstrated any special belief in me or felt that I could grow into an elite player. Then, out of nowhere during the last year of both our careers, he started referring to me as a Hall of Famer. Which I appreciate, but believe me, he never said anything like that to me or my contract agent, Ethan Locke, when we were in contract talks. Quite the contrary. In fact, I think one of Ernie's statements to us was, "I'm more comfortable paying a twenty-nine-year-old corner-back than a twenty-five-year-old running back." Running backs are judged on their production, and GM's are judged on Ws and Ls. But the franchise limitations go beyond Accorsi. The facts are clear: Three play-off wins across seventeen seasons is not a record the Giants or I can really boast about.

SUPER BOWL

In early 1999 I started to work with a man who would become one of my best friends as well as my business manager, Mark Lepselter. I had met Lep a couple years before that, in 1997, through an offensive lineman for the Giants named Jerry Reynolds.

"Hey, Lep," Reynolds had said to Mark, "there's this guy on the team I think you should check out. He's not your usual football player."

Mark became Ronde's business manager too, and eventually we became partners. Lep is my Jerry Maguire. He shows me the money. Every NFL player has ten-percenters buzzing around him, but Lep is different. He was interested in what I was doing off the field. He intuitively connected with the idea that I am "not just a football player." He took that ball and ran with it.

It could not have been easy at first. I wasn't a name back then.

My work experience doing anything but football was pretty much nil. To get my foot in the door in broadcasting, we offered my voice and analysis gratis to the bottom rung of the media world: late-night radio and the five a.m. local news.

I woke up at four a.m. during the off-season to be able to do it. I was the early morning sports anchor for the local CBS affiliate, Channel 2. Plus I made appearances on New York's premier sports-talk station, WFAN. At times it seemed insane to haul my body out of bed and trek out to Astoria to a radio studio. For free. I liked it exactly because I appeared at an off hour to an audience of cabbies and insomniacs.

Not yet ready for prime time, I had to start somewhere. The experience gave me a chance to get my feet wet in broadcasting without my mistakes having too much of an impact. A few times I committed the cardinal sin of radio: dead air. Me working in early morning radio had the same rationale as a Broadway show mounting an out-of-town preview run. I hoped it would represent a shakedown cruise for bigger and better things.

Lep brimmed with off-the-field ideas. Later on, Ronde and I started a series of children's books based on our experiences growing up and playing football together. Neither of us were writers. But our books came from the heart, and children (and parents) seemed to like them.

When I had the wild-ass impulse to say yes to some producers who wanted me to act in an off-Broadway play, Mark encouraged me.

Part of all this activity was simply plugging into the hot electrical socket of New York City. Ginny and I weren't sitting alone in our apartment. "If you're bored in New York, you're boring"—

so runs the anonymous wisdom. We weren't bored, and nobody called us boring.

My on-the-field life changed dramatically around that time too. For the last five games of the 1999 season, the Giants handed offensive play-calling duties to our quarterback coach, Sean Payton. Payton played as a quarterback himself at Eastern Illinois State, and he had coached a few college teams and the Eagles before winding up with the Giants. With him calling the plays under Jim Fassel, we started to score points. The next season, in 2000, the Giants made Sean the team's offensive coordinator.

I liked Sean tremendously. He was young, good-natured, exactly on my wavelength. He used to shack up overnight at the stadium, studying film and sleeping on a couch in his office. His wife Beth told me she never saw him for more than a couple of hours a day during the season.

The late Peter Drucker and some other business gurus pioneered a bottom-up management style that revolutionized corporations in the modern era. The core idea was that instead of managers issuing edicts from on high, they were to see their function as doing whatever necessary to make their employee's jobs easier and more productive.

Sean Payton grasped this idea on an intuitive level. Years later, when the post-Katrina New Orleans Saints won their division and made a storybook attempt at an NFL title in 2006, a reporter asked Sean to share his philosophy of coaching.

"No big secret," he replied. "I just recognize what my guys do good and let them do it."

Despite the mumbo-jumbo mouthings of sports analysts, football is not that complicated. If Reggie Bush is good at catching short passes and running misdirection plays, why would you want him plowing right between the tackles? Sean transformed the Giants offense in the 2000 season, a precursor of what he would do six years later in New Orleans.

With the Saints in 2006, Payton used a twin running-back offense with Deuce McAllister and Reggie Bush. Back in 2000 with the Giants, he utilized me and the Giants' just-drafted power back, Ron Dayne.

Thunder and lightning. I think Sean actually coined the phrase, referring to Ron's and my different running styles. Ron was thunder as the bigger, heavier back, and he'd run downhill. I was lightning because I was quick, and I'd more than likely go around the outside.

"When I think 'thunder,'" Sean told reporters, "I send in Ron, and when I think 'lightning,' I send in Tiki."

Sean also went to head coach Jim Fassel with what I can only characterize as a blinding glimpse of the obvious.

"Jim, every time Tiki gets his hands on the ball he's gaining six or seven yards." Sean's conclusion? "We've got to find a way to get the ball to Tiki more."

Recognize what your players do well and let them do it.

That year I emerged from the shadow of being a third-down back. That year I started to achieve at the level I'd always hoped I would. That year, under Payton's guidance, I began to step up from being a good running back to being a great one.

Could I have done it before that time? If an offensive genius such as Sean Payton had been around when I first signed with the Giants in 1997, would I have stepped up that much earlier? Did the team not realize what it had at the beginning? Had I been wasted and ill-used my first three seasons in the NFL?

I don't think so. The Eagles (the band, not the football team) have a song lyric: "It wasn't really wasted time." I spent those first three years learning the game at the professional level. I faced the Hill with Greg Comella and the gang-tackle death-plunge of the punt return. I studied film until I fell asleep. There were a hundred different elements over those years that helped make me able to take advantage of the opportunity Sean presented me.

But once those elements clicked, I needed a Sean Payton to recognize them. I actually think that the ability to respond with enthusiasm to someone else's potential is almost as rare as talent itself. I owe a lot to Sean Payton and the other gatekeepers who've helped me throughout my career.

Part of it was that Sean related so well to players on a personal level. He was easygoing and always joking around. I realized he was a different sort of coach on the practice field during training camp in Albany that first summer he acted as offensive coordinator.

We were running drills on a pleasantly cool August afternoon. I was present and accounted for, but my mind was racing with a hundred different urgencies. That's the way I've always been, ever since I was a little kid. "I get away only in my mind," was how Boyz II Men used to sing it. I must have looked zoned out, because Sean called to me.

"Uh, Tiki? Could you look a little bit more like you're with us? Maybe a little less bored, please?"

His tone was light, one dude giving another dude a hard time. Dayne and our QB Kerry Collins laughed.

"All right, Coach," I said. "I'll give it a try."

As a manager, you can always get more out of people with a playful, give-and-take manner, rather than with an overbearing

"I'm-the-boss" seriousness. Peter Drucker would agree with me. Your goal as a manager, he said, is to help your people do their jobs.

Sean had all these ideas that summer on how we could evolve into a new kind of offense. The Giants had been employing a typical NFC East grind-it-out-style football: running between the tackles and throwing out-and-outs on third downs.

"We're going to be doing something different this year," Sean announced in training camp. We called them "dick-'em plays": misdirection plays, confusing the defense with motion, tossing the ball outside the ends.

The new scheme fit my style. All of a sudden I didn't have to run between the tackles to be a running back—I could run a misdirection play: take three steps, cut back. Everyone blocks as though we're going one way, then we switch and cut off the back side.

If it panned out the way we planned, it would be just me one-on-one in the open field against a single safety or a cornerback. Just how I like it.

Thunder and lightning. Me and Ron. Neither one of us was the designated starter. We just split time. I didn't feel competitive with Ron. His style was different from mine. I've always been complemented by a straight-ahead bulldozer style of back. Brandon Jacobs played that role in the last couple years of my career.

Thunder is fine. Thunder can make you jump. It scares the shit out of dogs. But lightning can kill you. I prefer lightning.

That year, 2000, I had my first thousand-yard season. But more importantly, that was the year the Giants went to the Super Bowl.

Kansas City Chiefs owner Lamar Hunt supposedly named the NFL championship game in the late 1960s, after he saw his children playing with the Wham-O company's Super Ball, a new toy that was all the rage back then. The way a Super Ball zings around in unexpected ricochets always reminded me of the Super Bowl itself. A Super Ball is hard to catch hold of, just as it's difficult to nab a Super Bowl ring. A lot of the players still refer to the game by the name former football commissioner Pete Rozelle used: The Big One.

Toward the end of the 2000 season, the Giants were in the hunt for the NFL championship. I was playing well. On November 22 of that year, Coach Fassel made his famous announcement guaranteeing we would make the play-offs that year. Three and a half weeks after that, I broke my ulna, a bone in my left forearm.

"You're going to miss six weeks," said Dr. Russell Warren, the Giants team physician.

"Doc, you have to come up with something better than that." There was no way I was going to be left out of the effort to make good on Coach Fassel's guarantee, as well as out of the fast-and-furious run at the Lombardi Trophy.

The solution? I played wounded, with a soft cast on my arm. It just wasn't in me to lie down. I'll never do it. In a strange way, I know I'll always be successful, because you can't fail if you don't quit.

I broke my arm in the Dallas game on December 17, 2000. Six weeks later, on January 28, 2001, I started in Super Bowl XXXV.

To get there, we had to blow past the Eagles and the Vikings, and blow past them we did—the Vikes especially. After disposing of Philly, we faced Minnesota at home for the National Football Conference championship on January 14, 2001.

I always enjoyed bringing some motivation into the locker

room. I would use a prop, scrawl messages on the board, anything to give my teammates a boost before a game.

Before this one, I got a Randy Moss replica jersey ("No. 84") and had the logo of Super Bowl XXXV printed onto it. On top of that, I pinned a quote I cribbed from General Ulysses S. Grant: "The art of war is simple enough. Find out where your enemy is. Get to him as soon as you can. Strike at him as hard as you can and keep moving on." I left the whole tableau in the middle of the locker room where everyone could see it.

It must have worked. The game was a blowout. After only five offensive plays, we were ahead, 14–0. The second touchdown had come on a Kerry Collins pass to my best-friend fullback, Greg Comella. I was overjoyed for him to get a TD reception in a conference championship. At the half, the score stood at 34–0, and we ended the game winning by a score of 41–0. The debacle was known as "forty-one-doughnut" in the Vikings locker room.

A lot had been written about us that year: that we weren't very good, that we had snuck into the play-offs, that we were the worst team ever to advance that far. After the game, a jubilant Wellington Mara faced the press.

"Today we proved that we're the worst team to ever win the National Football Conference championship," he said. "I'm happy to say that in two weeks we're going to try to become the worst team ever to win the Super Bowl."

It was not to be. In Super Bowl XXXV, we played the Baltimore Ravens at Tampa's Raymond James Stadium—Ronde's home arena. Our offense got completely stuffed by the Ravens dominating defense, almost as badly as we had stuffed the Vikings two weeks before.

One indication of how the game went is that a defensive player received the Super Bowl MVP award—a relatively rare event. Offensive MVPs outnumber defensive MVPs by a ratio of five to one. But Pro Bowl linebacker Ray Lewis deserved the accolade. I was on the receiving end of a few of his teeth-loosening hits.

Losing in the Super Bowl represented the bitterest of the bitter, but also the sweetest of the sweet. Sweet because we were good enough that season to make it all the way. Bitter because we played badly in the championship. I don't think many players in the game today really appreciate how rare it is to make it to the Big One. At every step of the way, chance can intervene, and formerly favored teams can fall due to injuries, bad calls, or just the crazy way a foot-ball bounces.

There were a few bright spots that day in Tampa. My twenty-seven-yard run in the second quarter set us up to score, but on the next play Ravens cornerback Chris McAlister snagged an interception. Drive snuffed. The Giants had five turnovers that day. Our only score came on a Ron Dixon kickoff return in the third quarter. Incredibly, on the next play Jermaine Lewis of the Ravens returned our kickoff all the way too. It wasn't football, it was Ping-Pong.

After the bitterness of the defeat subsided, I still felt the satisfaction of achieving a thousand-yard season. I had no idea that in five years I'd be rushing for more than 1,800 yards. All I knew was that I was heading the right way. Up.

Then I lost it.

The ball, I mean. Or rather, I lost my ability to hold on to the ball. In 2000, our Super Bowl season, I fumbled nine times and lost three. The next year I fumbled eight times and lost two, and in both of the succeeding years I fumbled nine times and lost six.

Written down on the page, the numbers don't look severe, especially since in those years I had in excess of two hundred touches each season. But at the time, losing the ball loomed large. The turnover is the absolute crux of football. You simply cannot win games coughing up the ball to the other team. Your offense is on the field, you're driving, and with an interception or a fumble all of a sudden it's as though the whole team has crashed into a wall.

Even though I gained more than 1,500 all-purpose yards every year, my 2000–2003 seasons became tagged with a two-word mark of Cain: "Tiki fumbles." Seared in my memory of that time are the boos echoing through Giants Stadium. It was horrible. I couldn't get out from underneath my fumbling. My career was taking off, but it was as though it had a lead weight attached to it.

I was reckless with the ball. I still had the old mentality from high school and college, of being quick and agile and cutting back all the time. But I was an every-down back now. And fancy footwork didn't cut it (literally) when I was plowing through a line of scrimmage. In the scrum of a pileup, the ball gets knocked out very easily. I was exposed. I handled the ball much more during the 2000–2003 seasons, but I was also more susceptible to fumbling. And that's all the commentators focused on.

Back to square one. My pro career had taken off like a rocket, crashed to the Earth with my injury, took off a second time when Sean Payton arrived, and was now in a tailspin once again.

In the middle of this period, I violated a cardinal rule in professional sports: *Thou shalt not comment on thy teammate's deal.* In the 2002 off-season, I commented.

Pro Bowl defensive end Michael Strahan, who had just set the

single-season sack record with twenty-two and a half, was in contract negotiations with the Giants. The team offered Michael a
seven-year, $58 million deal, with a $17 million signing bonus split
over two years. Strahan turned the offer down. He didn't like the
split. He wanted the whole $17 million up front. He threatened to
leave the team.

On Saturday, March 17, Michael was quoted in *Newsday* saying
he didn't expect to be a Giant in 2003. He took issue with the split
bonus, citing me by name.

"[The Giants negotiators] say, 'We did the same with [Jason]
Sehorn and Tiki, and you have to go by our word.' No one's word
means anything in this business. In football the only thing you're
guaranteed is your bonus."

Well, yes. He was right. During my contract negotiations after
our Super Bowl season, we hammered out a deal for a six-year, $25
million extension. I agreed to split my signing bonus over the
course of two years.

It's hard to understand why this is crucial unless you are familiar with the arcane world of salary caps in the NFL. By agreeing to
split my $7 million bonus, I allowed the Giants room under the
salary cap to sign other talent that they might not have been able to
sign if I had insisted on a lump sum. Amani Toomer had also split
his bonus payment, and as Michael noted, so had Jason Sehorn.

I had a promise from Wellington Mara that the bonus money
would be there in the second year. I accepted that promise. His word
held plenty of meaning to me, because I knew he represented the
gold standard of integrity in the league.

Michael had a point. The only guaranteed money in football is
the signing bonus. When you read of the huge contracts paid out

over the course of several years, you have to understand that if a player gets injured or cut, those millions vanish. You don't get paid if you don't perform.

I had played my whole professional career with the Giants. They were my team. I felt loyalty to Bob Tisch and Wellington Mara, to the tradition of the team, and to the Giants franchise. This was, I realize now, somewhat of an old-fashioned view.

A lot of players come into the NFL with what I can only call a modular view of the game. They see themselves as modules who can plug in pretty much anywhere. They might play for a specific team, but they don't care who the owners are or about the business health of the franchise. They don't feel any buy-in. It's basically just a job for them.

I was always friendly with Michael. We got along well. I had played my whole professional career with him too. Because of my friendship with Bob and Wellington, I cared about the New York Giants and the overall viability of the league. I saw what I perceived to be the wider picture, wherein isolated self-interest threatened the game that I loved and that had given so much to me and my family.

I've heard people say this attitude makes me a sucker, a patsy, a house slave. I've been called a lot of names. But I felt the way I felt, so I spoke out.

"I don't know if Michael realizes how much $17 million is," I told the *New York Post*. What I meant was how much $17 million impacted the salary cap numbers.

I probably should have stopped there, but I went on. "He's already the highest-paid defensive player in the league. He's already making more than most quarterbacks."

I reacted to Michael's situation as both a Giant and a Giants fan.

Looking back, it might have been better if I had observed the cardinal rule and kept my mouth shut. The issue spiraled out of control in the press. Michael insisted that his position had been mischaracterized.

Michael stayed with the team, continuing his Hall of Fame career. The dustup didn't influence our face-to-face relations at all. We were as we always had been, cordial and professional. Today Michael and I remain good friends.

The whole issue is now dead and long gone. I did take away a few lessons. One is that I still believe loyalty and team pride remain crucial facets of the game even at the pro level. I can hear the cynics laughing, but it's true. I had Pro Bowl–level seasons because, in part, loyalty to my team motivated me. It speaks to the fundamental quality of meaning. In order to do something well, you have to find the meaning behind doing it.

Also, beginning with the Strahan controversy and extending to my later pro career, I've been consistently criticized for speaking out. *Who is Tiki Barber to talk?* It's a sentiment I would encounter with increasing frequency in the years to come, and it has always frustrated me. I didn't notice any gag-order clause in my Giants contract eliminating my right of free speech. You sign me, you sign the whole package, mouth and all.

Besides, I found the "shut up and play ball" attitude demeaning, insulting, and just plain wrong. It portrays football players as a crew of dumb-fuck lugs, unable to formulate coherent thoughts into full sentences. It tries to put me in a box.

But maybe part of the reason I questioned Michael was that I was questioning myself so much. During that period, I had become increasingly rattled by the constant chorus of "fumbalaya!"

that was sounding whenever I hit the field at Giants Stadium.

I don't think anyone who hasn't experienced what it feels like to be booed by eighty thousand fans can gauge the emotional impact. There were times when I felt lower than dog shit. Old doubts came winging back in. *Too small, too small . . . to play football.* Because I was actually running the ball well and putting up big total-yardage numbers, I had a deep sense of frustration.

Maybe deeper than I realized. Mouthing off about a teammate's contract wasn't the only sign. Despite my "fiery-tempered" name, I normally keep a totally even keel off the field. But as Ronde, Lep, and I walked down a Chicago street one evening in the off-season, I almost exploded out of my usual calm self.

"Hey, Tiki," a bystander called out. He was a fat slob of a guy, pretty drunk, backed up by three twentysomething friends. We were on Rush Street, in Chicago's so-called "Viagra Triangle" of nightclubs and bars.

"Hey, how it's going?" I muttered, powering straight by the dude. I didn't want to get into it with him. My spider-sense tingled and somehow I knew that he was some sort of wiseass.

The slob didn't disappoint. "Why don't you learn to hold on to the fucking football, asshole?"

I felt my trigger click. Just as I was about to turn on him and get up into his grille, Lep lunged forward. Mark's a big, squared-off guy, and he put a look of terror on the faces of Fat Slob and the Twentysomethings that was awesome to behold.

Ronde wanted to get at the guy too. No blows were exchanged, just a quick, chest-beating face-off and we were gone. I didn't look back to check if the four guys had wet their pants, but given Lep's monster rage, anything was possible.

I thanked my lucky stars Ronde and Lep had been with me. They both had the same sense of knowing the guy was going to crack wise, and they stepped in to prevent anything from happening that might have made the *Chicago Trib* the next morning.

Lep told me later he never had seen me so angry. My eyes were open so wide, he said, that he could see the whites.

"I'll never forget how pissed you were," Lep said, laughing and shaking his head in the aftermath.

I calmed down and gave myself a reality check. I'd had a lot worse things screamed at me during my career. The fact that this one anonymous drunk with a tossed-off comment had nearly moved me to assault meant that the fumbalaya situation was getting to me.

Somehow I had to solve it.

Soon after the swirl of controversy surrounding me and Strahan, and in the midst of fumbalaya, something came along to put it all in perspective—not only those particular situations, but all of football and all of life. In the summer of 2002 Ginny and I had our first child, a son.

AJ. Atiim Junior. When he was born, Ginny and I cast around for names, and I didn't necessarily want to have my son living in my shadow. But in the end, my friend Mark Zimmerman convinced me of the inevitable.

"You know that whatever you name your son, he's always going to be Tiki Junior," Zimm said.

I look into my son AJ's eyes, or into the eyes of my son Chason, who was born less than two years later, and I see enjoyment of life and playfulness. I see curiosity, and love, and all those things, but in one way I am looking at them and deep down in my mind is this bedrock thought: I don't ever want to disappoint them. I want to be an honorable man because that's what I want them both to be.

So having a child is a great motivator. I know some people who say, "Procreate and die," and that you lose your edge once you have children, but that didn't happen to me. I became more determined than ever to live my life a certain way.

Starting a family underscored the importance I've always placed on finding motivation in my life. For the vast majority of people out there, having children is the main element that lends meaning and depth and importance to what they do and how they do it. That characteristic runs straight through from the CEO of a company to a guy who empties the wastebaskets. It's the reason you get out of bed in the morning. Not just for the money to buy them shoes and put food on the table. But to be the kind of person your child can look up to.

In *As Good As It Gets*, I always remember the moment when Jack Nicholson wins Helen Hunt's heart by giving her this compliment: "You make me want to be a better man." Apart from everything, apart from the joy and laughter and love AJ and Chason have brought into my life, having children made me want to be a better man.

Michael Strahan stayed on as a Giant, but we lost another key person after our dismal 4–12 finish in the 2003 season. The Giants fired the man who had been, up to that time, my first and only pro-ball head coach. Jim Fassel had learned to love me as a player, and I had learned to love him as a coach. Not that we ever articulated our mutual sentiment. The closest we came was when I encountered Jim's daughter Jana in the hallway at the stadium one afternoon.

"I can't thank you enough for all that you do for my dad," she said. "You literally helped him keep his job."

Jim Fassel did the best he could with the talent the team had.

"Coach Coughlin and Tiki will not get along." That was the buzz in the air after the Giants announced they were replacing Jim Fassel with former Jacksonville Jaguars head coach Tom Coughlin.

More buzz: "Jim Fassel was lax with Tiki." "Jim never enforced the little things." "When Tiki fumbled, Jim would never take him out."

How could Fassel take me out? During some games, I produced the bulk of the offense.

It didn't matter. I hadn't even sat down and spoken with Tom, and already everyone had us at loggerheads. But as it played out, Coach Coughlin had an impact on my performance that no one could have predicted.

Straightforward. That's how I found Coughlin when I first met him. In the sense that he was direct, and also in the sense that he tended to be extremely goal-oriented.

"Here's what we'd like you to accomplish next year," Coughlin stated. Then he described a laundry list of my offensive duties, goals such as keeping my average yardage up, catching quick passes like five-yard outs or eight-yard posts, performing pass-rush blocking for Eli—basically, duties I had been performing all along.

I said okay.

Jerald Ingram was at the meeting too. Coach Ingram worked with Tom Coughlin first at Boston College and then with the Jaguars, and Tom had brought him along to the Giants as our running-back coach. During Ingram's college playing days in the early eighties, he had been a fullback at Michigan.

"How much do you bench press?" Coach Ingram asked me.

"Fuck if I know, Coach," I said. I had never really thought about it.

But Ingram persisted. "How about your curl? How much can you curl?"

"I honestly don't know."

"I guess what I'm trying to get at is this," Coach Ingram went on. "How strong are you in your upper body?"

"I don't really work out my upper body," I told him.

Ever since Cave Spring High, I had always done some sort of conditioning training. But I never really did any strength training. I was quick. For a long time, that was enough—for high school, for college, for my entry into the NFL. What Coach Ingram told me, in so many words, was that being in top physical shape wasn't all I needed anymore. To counteract my tendency to lose the ball, I would have to get stronger.

"You need to start working on your biceps and your chest," Coach Ingram said.

Coach Coughlin suggested that I start carrying the ball a little higher on my body. Not in the crook of my arm, the way I had done during my freewheeling days as a cutback, open-field style of runner.

"Up there," he explained, gesturing to my chest. That way, I had more of my body surface in contact with the ball. Tom also suggested that I hold it vertically, instead of horizontally. Again, more surface contact.

It's funny, but I don't remember the word "fumble" ever being spoken at that meeting. It didn't have to be. Everyone knew what everybody was talking about. That two-word judgment: "Tiki fumbles."

The situation reminded me of my days with the Cavaliers, when Coach Mack laid out my choices for me. Bulk up or play a minor role. Now it was, "Get stronger or you'll continue to have trouble holding on to the ball."

But even with two coaches telling me what I had to do, I'm not sure if I would have actually followed through. I might have changed my way of carrying the ball. That was easy enough. But the strength training was another issue.

I had tried strength training before but never stuck at it long enough. I just didn't see the payoff clearly. After my discussion with Coach Ingram, I probably would have done the same thing I always did: gone into the weight room a few times, done some desultory work, and then let it slide. That was what had always happened to me before.

Joe Carini wouldn't let it happen again.

Mark Lepselter found him for me. Carini was a perennial contestant in New Jersey World's Strongest Man competitions. He didn't lift for definition, for the kind of ripped and cut muscles that win body-builder competitions. He lifted for power.

"Go see this guy in Paterson," Lep said to me, after I told him Jerald Ingram wanted me to work on my upper body. "His place is a shit-hole, but he's the best there is."

Paterson, New Jersey. Once one of the manufacturing centers of the Northeast, now fallen on hard times. I couldn't believe it the first time I journeyed to Carini's gym. Actually, "gym" gives the place too much credit. I found myself in a dingy-ass room underneath a Russian Orthodox church in a run-down neighborhood of Paterson. I felt like Rocky. Every time they held a service I could smell the incense from upstairs.

I'm a professional football player. I am the starting running back for the New York Giants. What am I doing in this hellhole of a gym?

Joe didn't bother with niceties. He's a caricature of a person, five-eight, 350 pounds, forty-eight years old, a repeat winner on the weight-lifting circuit.

He immediately made me start lifting like a power lifter, like "the world's strongest man" power lifter. There weren't any Nautilus machines, elliptical trainers, or lattes anywhere around the little gym. What he had me doing was picking up dead-weight bags. I carried canvas bags from one corner of the dingy, ill-lit room to the other.

I also did a whole spectrum of squats, strange body configurations I had never encountered before. These were movements that generate power. They weren't like reps. Fifteen reps on a specific muscle group help to make you look ripped. But it won't give you power. Joe had me doing squats and lifts for only one or two reps. One push, another push, and then I was done for a set.

Joe Carini made me into a powerful running back. I was always fast and explosive. But Carini gave me a missing piece of the puzzle. Strength. Now I started breaking tackles. And I found myself better able to hold on to the football despite contact.

And oddly enough, I got faster, even though I gained around ten pounds of muscle. Because one of the big components of speed, outside of stride length and stride frequency, is strength.

Joe Carini was bad for my golf game—because the muscles I developed constricted my swing—but he was miraculous for my running game. Even more important, the lifting I did with Joe down there in the Paterson basement transformed my whole performance mentality.

I was lifting obscene amounts of weight. Carini had me leg-pressing 1,100 pounds. I remember the first time he told me that he wanted me to do that kind of lift.

"You've got to be fucking kidding me," I responded. "There is no way I am doing this."

As I was approaching these crazy weights, I remember the constant drumming of my inner voice: *"I can't do this, I can't do this, I can't do this!"*

A self-fulfilling prophecy. The negativity would not allow me to do it. In fact, it forced me to be unable to do it.

But Joe got in my face. "Come on, Tiki!" he said. "You got to get your mind right. We're gonna do this!"

He looked like he would explode if he didn't get me to lift a particular weight at a specific time. "All right, man, I'll do it."

And I was able to do it. These were loads that I never imagined I could do. I continued to get stronger and stronger. And as I did so, my mentality started to change.

Now my inner voice sang a different tune. *"I can do this. I have no doubt that I can do this."*

That mentality carried over to me as a football player. My newfound strength was part of it. After I trained with Carini, instead of linebackers putting a hit on me, I would put hits on them.

It was elementary physics once again. To overcome a force, meet it with an equal or superior force. Linebackers love to put moves straight out of the boxing ring on running backs. Smash-mouth, roundhouse-right moves. But when I smashed back at them, the force of their blows was negated. I might have known the general physics principle behind that, but Joe Carini helped me develop the strength to make it work on the playing field.

TIKI INTERVIEWS TIKI

Q Would you play again if the Giants had a new coach?

A No. The bottom line is that my football career has run its course. I can't tell you what a weight has been lifted off my shoulders since I left football. All my family and friends have remarked upon it. I'm a different person, looser, more relaxed. I am there for my wife and kids in ways I could never be when I was playing. Plus I am tremendously excited about the work I am doing for NBC on *Today*. That's my life now. Playing football is in the rearview for me. The game itself will always fascinate me, which is why I signed on to *Football Night in America*. But there are days when the memory of actually playing doesn't even cross my mind. It's that remote.

GAME FACE

When I hear the sound of offensive lineman Richie Seubert throwing up, I know it's game time.

"We must be ready to go," I say to myself, as Seubert ralphs into a garbage can in the bathroom.

Regular as clockwork, Richie can be depended on to lose his cookies just before we head out onto the field. As game-day rituals go, it's not that rare—Richie's fellow guard Chris Snee and my man Plaxico Burress have been known to get green around the gills too—but throwing up before kickoff illustrates the intensity of game day.

Professional football is an exercise in intensity, and one way to handle intensity is to devise rituals, to better be able to channel stress.

I've got my own pregame ritual, not quite as dramatic as Richie's. I fall asleep.

Well, not always. But surprisingly often. As the clock ticks down to kickoff, I start to get anxious. I'm excited to go get into it, but I'm nervous at the same time. Whenever I get that way, excited-nervous, I become sleepy. Often I go back into the equipment room, because nobody really comes in there before games.

I sit and just chill. Try to clear my mind of anything and everything that has been in my head. Nervousness makes my stomach feel all-encompassing, as though it's taking over my body. I relax and—sometimes, not always—fall asleep.

The next thing I know, I hear an assistant coach or someone shouting out in the hall.

"All right, all right—it's time to get out there and get it done!"

I snap back awake. I feel so refreshed and ready that it's unbelievable.

I wouldn't recommend this particular ritual. But that's the point. Most game-day rituals are strictly idiosyncratic and personal. Somebody else might pace and listen to hip-hop on earphones, full volume. I lie down with my feet up.

Here's game day for me. The general rule is to arrive at the stadium two hours early. Entering the parking lot, seeing the stadium, coming into the locker room: that's when your nerves start to come up a little bit. You're not exactly panting in anxiety, but you start thinking about how the game's going to be. You start visualizing what is about to happen.

When guard Ron Stone was a Giant, he used to fix me a pregame meal. Ron has six kids, so he knows how to feed a crowd. After one of his awesome waffles, I'd have some pasta, too, for dessert. Lots of carbs for the pregame meal.

That long before kickoff, the stadium is still pretty much empty.

It has a deserted, ghost-town feel to it. Some of the guys take laps around the field. I don't do any of that. I sit in front of my locker, take off my suit, strip down to shorts and a T-shirt, and maybe listen to music. Light jazz, sometimes classic R & B. If I don't have the headphones on, I can hear the muted sounds of everybody else's tunes, lots of rock, heavy metal, and rap, all jangled together.

The uniform of a professional football player is the biggest pain in the ass you could ever imagine. That's especially true for running backs like me, since defenders are forever grabbing, tugging, and clutching at us. Because of that, my uniform must be as tight and sleek as possible. I know a lot of people (women, mostly) talk about the vanity of the skintight NFL uniform, but to me it's strictly utility.

My waist is thirty-two inches, but the uniform pants I wear are thirty short. A twelve-year-old could probably wear these pants and feel comfortable in them. The material stretches, so they're not oppressively tight, but there's nothing for a linebacker to grab onto, either.

I never wear sleeves. I always wear a summer uniform shirt, even when it's ten degrees outside. Over the years, my jersey has shrunk down to a size forty. I used to wear a forty-four, which was itself pretty tight. It's all in the service of never giving my opponents an inch of extra fabric by which to snag me. The bigger I get, the smaller the jersey.

You know the line: If you like to eat sausage you probably shouldn't watch it being made. Well, if you like football, you probably shouldn't watch a pro footballer stuff himself into his uniform, either. Unless you're looking for a few laughs.

The problem is that because the jersey is so tight across the chest, the fabric tends to squeeze your shoulder pads together like an accordion. With the pads closed, I've got a very small hole to cram myself into. I have to fit my head and my arms through a space about the size of a grapefruit.

I stand on one side, pulling and stretching my jersey. It's hard. I have to muscle myself into it. Then I do it again on the other side, pull it up, hold it there, put one arm in, put the other arm in, grab it, get snagged on both elbows, jam my head into the hole.

It's excruciating. I feel like a contortionist. The only thing that alleviates the embarrassment is that there are forty-five guys in the immediate vicinity going through the same spastic dance.

But then, once I'm in, I'm in. It's like magic. The uniform conforms to you like a second skin. The total weight of jersey, pants, pads, shoes, and helmet is around eight pounds. But somehow, the whole package makes you feel lighter, not heavier.

In fact, you start to feel . . . invincible. It doesn't happen with a practice uniform. When you put on the game uniform, nothing in the world can touch you. There's a force field between you and your enemy, like the ones Sulu used to drop in front of the Starship Enterprise.

The uniform itself is just spandex and rip-stop nylon and stamp-formed polymer plastic, but somehow you convince yourself that it will protect you and give you the strength to dominate your opponents. It's just a trick of the mind, of course, but it's as real a feeling as any I've ever encountered.

I'm not the only one checking my look in the mirror. Forty-plus game-day divas stand around and fuss in front of their own locker mirrors. We're all making sure our shirts are tucked in just right, or that our socks are perfect.

Geraldine Barber and me and Ronde in the mid-1970s

Our first day of first grade

Ronde and I have always been inseparable . . . and, in the old days, hard to tell apart.

Here we are with our mom at the Cave Springs High School graduation, June 1993—I'm on the right, wearing the valedictorian medal. (What do you think of our Carl Lewis fades?)

And here we are at our mom's graduation from business school.

Before a game at my locker—I had the coveted corner real estate.

Jerry Pinkus

Nothing tops playing in the Super Bowl.

Me, Ginny, her dad and mom, and our sons, Chason (left) and AJ (right)

Michael Jurick

Me and Ronde at our first Pro Bowl together

Courtesy of Ginny Barber

I'll never forget meeting Shimon Peres, a chance encounter that changed my life.

At the Wailing Wall with our good friends. From left to right: me, Amy Lepselter, Mark Lepselter, Ginny, and Kenny Cardona.

Courtesy of Ginny Barber

Me and my boy Greg Comella soakin' up the sun

My beautiful wife, Ginny, threw me a big bash for my thirtieth birthday.

Courtesy of Ginny Barber

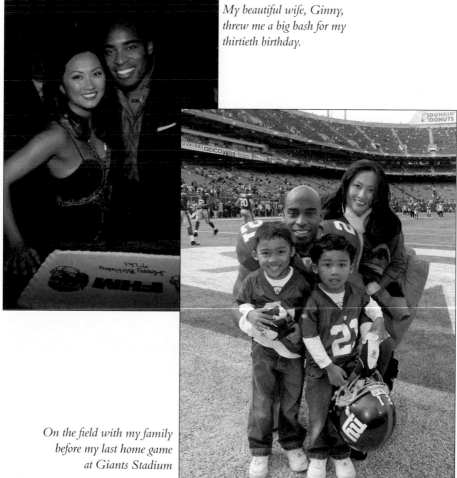

On the field with my family before my last home game at Giants Stadium

Evan Pinkus

This photo appeared in the New Yorker *and I never heard the end of it.*

It sounds ridiculous, and it shouldn't have any relevancy, but it does. The simple fact is if you feel good, you play well. And you have to look good to feel good. All that fussing and primping is one way to calm the jitters, but it's also a bow to the fact that we're going out there in front of audiences numbering tens of millions.

The league works overtime to make sure that the uniform is, well, uniform. Everybody has their own style, so everyone is constantly trying to modify the standard package in ways they believe make them look better. Little modifications, such as a pair of socks worn a bit differently, or a wristband doubled up.

To counter this, the league employs uniform police—for the Giants, former running back Joe Morris serves this function. He goes around during warm-ups with a clipboard and checklist, looking for violations. Low socks, no way. Shirt untucked, uh-uh. Do-rag with a logo from your favorite restaurant, no way. Joe cites violators, and he makes sure the infractions are corrected by the time the teams take the field.

It's all about control. Our appearance has to appeal to a vast continent of people, a lot of them highly conservative. The look, the professionalism, is part of the total package. The NFL, to its credit, understands that. It's why the league has a $3.5 billion television package. Put the NFL on TV in any market anywhere in this country, and people know they will get the same familiar product.

It's hard to argue with success. I remember our opening day last season, a Sunday night game against the Colts. Up against us on TV was a docudrama called *The Path to 9/11*. A serious, important look at what led up to the attacks on the World Trade Center and the Pentagon. Thirteen million people watched it. Twenty-one million watched the Giants versus the Colts.

Or check this out, a listing from Google of the top news stories the day after Peyton Manning and the Indianapolis Colts won the 2006 AFC championship game. The aspect that is interesting to me is the number of related stories filed on each subject.

Hope for more effective Serbian coalition (all 490 related)
Iraq War under scrutiny in U.S. presidential race (all 1,769 related)
Scavengers grab cargo from stricken ship (all 529 related)
O'Loan confirms collusion claims (all 208 related)
Suicide car bomber kills 3 Pakistani troops (all 116 related)
Iranian cleric attacks president (all 862 related)
Car bombs blast Baghdad market, killing 67 (all 310 related)
Manning is the Man (all 2,579 related)

In a day of bombings, shipwrecks, scandals, and political developments, by far the most news stories filed on any subject were about a football game.

The National Football League has grown into the most popular sports spectacle in America. In Roman times, the idea was to keep the public happy by giving them "bread and circuses"—meaning food and entertainment. Nowadays pro football players are the Roman gladiators.

The NFL isn't just part of American culture; to a large degree it *is* American culture. It's ingrained in people's minds in a symbolic way, just like Mom and apple pie. No one else in the world plays football the way we do. And no one else watches it the way we do. The sleek, sophisticated, professional surface is a fundamental part of it.

I never got cited by Joe Morris. My uniform was always impeccably within bounds. But I do have one uniform quirk. My shoes.

I put all my individuality into my kicks. For the last four or five years of my professional career, all my shoes were designed specifically for me. I can't share a style with anyone else.

This started in 2002. The official NFL style—the shoe rules that are enforced by the uniform police—required that teams designate themselves as either a white- or black-shoe team and wear shoes of only those shades, accented only by black or the team color.

Our equipment director, Joey Skiba, stopped me in the hall outside the locker room one day. "I've got these cool shoes I want you to look at," he said.

We were a white-shoe team at the time. The shoes that Joey showed me didn't have any white on them at all. They were silver.

"These are great," I told him. "Maybe we could do some red on the heel, make it look as though they have flames coming out of them."

So Joey and Reebok came up with a shoe for me. The soles were incandescent red. I thought about how that incandescence would look to a linebacker I had just blasted past, as he was chasing me down the field. Pretty cool, I thought. As far as the uniform police went, the shoes weren't kosher. They were a violation. I got away with wearing them simply because the league neglected to enforce its own rules.

No one else had that style of shoe except my brother. When the Giants changed to a black-shoe team for my last year, 2006, we came up with another version, with red accents, a red heel, and a shimmering platinum sole.

Vanity, saith the preacher, all is vanity. In size eleven and a half.

◆

Preseason, season, and off-season. Game day and game week. The rhythms of my life as a professional football player were always dictated by what time of year it was, what day, what was looming up ahead on Sunday.

My rituals and rhythms evolved over the course of my career. When I was young, in my early twenties, I would recover a lot sooner from the beating I took during a game. By Wednesday morning, say, three days after a game, I felt like I was 100 percent. Just in time for our first full day of practice. That was my "back-to-normal" marker, the point in time when I felt like saying, "I could play another game right now."

As I got older, the marker started to move inexorably toward later in the week. At first I was back to 100 percent by Wednesday afternoon. Then it was Wednesday night, after practice. By year ten, it got to be Friday evening before my inner voice told me, *I think I can play now.*

That's the struggle. I recover slower. That moving "I can play now" marker is like a physical correlative to my age. There's nothing I can do about it, no workout or regimen I can adopt to prevent it from happening.

I invite anyone who fails to appreciate this process to try it out for themselves. Run a gauntlet between two lines of very large, muscular professionals wielding baseball bats. See how you feel the next day, slugger. The next week. Do it, oh, 350 times over four months. See how that 100 percent marker moves for you, year by year.

As a result of the beating I took on the field, my preparation week before every game changed drastically. Gradually, over the years, I began to spend more and more time during the week in treatment to prepare myself for Sunday.

When I was a rookie, I never got any physical therapy at all. I never went in for massages, acupuncture, or anything of that nature. I didn't get worked on, because I didn't need to. My body was young. It was like a rubber band. Pull it, stretch it, torture it any which way. It didn't matter. I just snapped right back.

After my fourth season, though, I was ready for a change. I probably wasn't even aware of it mentally. Time slips by, your circumstance shifts, and at times you are slow to wake up to the new reality. Once again, I met a person who helped me through, just like Greg Comella did on the Hill, or Sean Payton on the field. Her name was Carol Tan, and she transformed the way I prepared to play football.

In June 2000, on a Sunday in the off-season, my wife Ginny and I were spending a lazy afternoon. This was before we had our sons AJ and Chason. (After they came along, I'm not sure Ginny and I could describe any of our afternoons as "lazy.") But on this early summer day in Manhattan, we decided we wanted to go to a spa.

We called around. The city was dead. Nothing was open. Except for one place in the Benjamin, a deluxe, boutique-style hotel on East 50th Street, so Ginny and I made an appointment.

We met the masseuse, Carol, who also managed the spa. She was an Asian lady who stood all of five-two. But when I shook hands with her, I could feel real strength and power in her grip.

"Are you ready?" she asked, after describing her deep-muscle approach.

Ginny and I looked at each other. Sure.

"Take your clothes off."

Carol worked on me for an hour that afternoon, and it was a transformative experience. It was, as the line in *Casablanca* goes, the beginning of a beautiful friendship. Ginny and I went back to the Benjamin routinely. Sometimes, during the season, I'd see Carol not once but twice a week. And there were times, after a particularly brutal game, when the massages needed to last not one hour, but three.

During a game or in practice, I would damage my muscles. The body's muscles are all aligned. Pull a muscle, stretch it too far, and when it retracts, it's out of alignment. A knot. Carol smoothed over the knot. Then she would dig into it, pushing on it, kneading it. Eventually the knot straightened back out to where it's supposed to be. At that point, the pull was not exactly healed. But at least it was aligned correctly.

One day she was massaging my hand. "When did you jam your finger?" she asked.

"What?" I said. "How did you know that?" I didn't tell her things, she just knew. During game week, I had these knots and pulls all over my body. Some of them I probably didn't even know about. But Carol found them. She could feel them.

After our Hill workout one day, Greg Comella and I talked about all our aches and pains. Greg's back is like a turtle shell, just a big arc of muscle. So I told him to go see Carol.

"That was the best massage I've ever gotten," he said when he came to the stadium the day after he visited her for the first time.

When we went to the Super Bowl later that year, Greg and I flew Carol down to Tampa. She worked on both of us almost every day we were down there. I'm older now, so I don't share a room with another player on the road, but that was my fourth year in, so I shared a room with Greg, mostly just because I liked talking to him. Carol brought her table in. She'd do bodywork on me, I'd drift off to sleep, and then she'd work on Greg.

One reason I've been healthy and effective as a football player is because I've learned how to take care of myself. My longevity as a running back—after my PCL injury I missed only two games in nine years—started when I just randomly met a masseuse at a New York spa. She ended up being the best massage therapist I've ever experienced. She's almost like a shrink for me. We can talk about anything. For six years, she acted as one of my healers.

Over my subsequent seasons in the NFL, I added more and more healers to my regimen, trying to stay ahead of the aging process. I've used massage, acupressure, acupuncture, and relaxation techniques, as well as the old standbys, heat and ice. The battery of therapies grew as my physical hurts became more pronounced after every game. It was like an arms race, football versus the healers.

The battle took a huge step forward in 2001, when I started seeing Dr. Robert DeStefano, a north Jersey chiropractor. I met him through Amani Toomer, who recovered extra quickly from a hamstring pull under Dr. Rob's care.

DeStefano works on athletes a lot and is one himself, participating in Iron Man competitions, which involve some of the most brutal workouts on Earth. He practices something called Active Release Technique, originally developed (and patented) by sports injury expert Dr. Michael Leahy.

Let's say I have a knot in my bicep, from one of those sledgehammer blows that are just a matter of course in football. When

Dr. Rob forces his finger through the locked-up muscle, he stretches out the tissue. The knot is unknotted.

It kills. When he is done with me, I feel great. But when he's working on me, I sometimes want to punch him.

"That's okay," Dr. Rob says. "All my clients feel that way."

You have all these tiny muscles in the body that control the big muscles. One small muscle in the hip might control your whole thigh. What Dr. Rob does differently from orthopedists and physical therapists is address the muscle lesion directly.

The year after we played the Super Bowl, we played the New York Jets in our annual preseason matchup. At that point in my career, I didn't have to play much in the dreaded preseason, when there is the greatest possibility of getting hurt in a meaningless contest. But this was the third preseason game, when the starters traditionally play the most.

It was midway through the second quarter, a few plays left before halftime. I knew I was about to be finished for the day. It's like in the military, when your tour of duty is almost up. You naturally become more superstitious that things might go wrong.

We ran an off-tackle sprint-out to the right. I got the ball, saw a hole, and cut upfield. Cool. Some running room. I felt the smallest little twinge right when I cut. Nothing big. I thought, *I'll worry about it when I get tackled. Maybe I'll go off and see what happened.*

We were at the forty yard line going out, so we had sixty yards to go. After the first cut, everything looked good. A defender came up, so I made another cut. I kept cutting around the defensive backs, going the opposite way. Every time I cut, I felt the twinge again. I became more and more tired. I received a key block from my receiver and angled across the open field.

With a play that started right, I had now wound up running down the left sideline. *God, yeah, this is nice. I'm gonna score. No doubt.* But I felt my leg start to get tight. *Oh, fuck. Let me just ease up a little bit.*

And then my hamstring pulled. I knew right away that it was bad. Suddenly, right in the middle of the run, I found myself walking. I was ten yards from the end zone. I tried to get out of bounds. *Okay,* I told myself, *I am just going to walk off.* But a back came up and knocked the ball out of my hand, and I fumbled.

Since it was the preseason, the fumble really didn't have any meaning. But it made the situation worse, since now not only did I not score, but I had this great run only to injure my hamstring and lose the ball.

I hobbled to the sidelines. I remember all the thoughts going through my mind. Regular season was two weeks away. Hamstrings take forever to heal. This was 2001, remember, right after we went to the Super Bowl. The Giants had great expectations for the season. Plus, that was the year that the NFL instituted a new Thursday night game to kick off the regular season. Bon Jovi would be playing. It would be a huge, nationally televised game. The fans were going to be crazy.

But I now had a pulled hamstring. *Are you kidding me? I'm going to miss the start of the season?*

I was crippled, but all I could think about was Bon Jovi.

Amani saved me by suggesting that I see Dr. Rob. DeStefano worked on me for an hour a day for the rest of the week, and then on a couple of days over the course of the next week. I played in the opening game against San Francisco on Thursday night. I wasn't full speed, but I was functional. I had a good game and even scored a touchdown.

I knew that learning how to take care of myself was one of the major components of being a good football player. But it was getting harder every year. As I've said, my platoon of healers kept growing. Carol Tan, Dr. Rob, Giants head trainer Ronnie Barnes and his staff. I felt like that creature on the *Star Trek* episode who needed every being on a whole planet just to keep itself alive.

I could look ahead and know that however hard my healers worked, eventually it would prove to be a losing battle. But I was doing all I could to stave off the inevitable.

In my mind, football is about trust. It's about your coaches being able to trust you as a player, to do the right thing and not fuck up. When they send in the play, when the quarterback calls it, you execute it.

It's also trust within yourself. Every game week we spend hours in preparation meetings, watching film, laying the groundwork for that week's opponent. It's tedious. It's as though you are back in school. Sets, patterns, looks. Starting on Wednesday and going through Friday, every game week, and then finishing off on Saturday with a low-impact walk-through.

On Monday we work out and watch game film from Sunday. If we win, occasionally the coach will give us Monday off. Tuesday is the NFL's official day off.

Wednesday begins our full drill. I show up at the Stadium early, eight a.m. or so. I usually have breakfast there: scrambled eggs, bacon, an English muffin. I'm in our first team meeting at 8:25. Coach Coughlin goes over our opponents for the upcoming game. He'll throw out some stats, name the opposing players to watch.

Then we split up, with offense and defense going into separate rooms for strategy meetings.

"These are the defensive fronts that they throw up," John Hufnagel, the offensive coordinator, will say, putting diagrams up on a visual. "This is our running game plan."

We go through the whole battery of running plays that we have in that week, and all the blocking assignments for each individual play. We move on to pass coverages. "These are the coverages that they play," Hufnagel says, running through them one by one. Then the blitz packages.

At that point, the offensive line leaves the room for their own meeting, and the receivers, running backs, and quarterbacks go through all the passes that we have in the playbook that week. By the end of this first series of meetings, we'll have detailed around fifty offensive plays.

Then we split up in individual groups: Running backs go to our room, wide receivers to theirs, quarterbacks to theirs. I've always believed that this is where the real work gets done, delving into the particulars, answering any questions anyone might have.

Once you split apart into individual position groups, the atmosphere loosens up. Coach Coughlin has you sitting up ramrod straight. But in the position meetings, it's more laid-back. Finny and I tilt our chairs back, putting our feet up on the table.

Talking with our running-back coach Jerald Ingram in these meetings is where most of the learning takes place. We start watching film, and we usually talk over the action.

"What are we going to do if this happens? Jerald, could you run that film back?"

Actually, of course, it hasn't been "film," for decades, it's been videotape or, lately, digital video, but for some reason—because the NFL is the most hidebound institution imaginable—everybody still calls it film.

One of the skills I had to develop as a football player is the ability to apply what I saw on film and transfer it to my play on the field. It's more difficult than you would think. The camera gives you a bird's-eye view of the action, but during the game you are locked into a boots-on-the-ground mentality. Over the years of watching film, I've gotten so comfortable with the bird's-eye perspective that I sometimes glance up during a play at the JumboTron screen in the stadium, just to check the position of the defenders.

Watching film, I start to see patterns and tendencies. More importantly, I begin to understand the wider strategy of the game.

This is crucial. It's the most difficult thing for a younger player to do. You start to understand why the coaches call a particular play in response to our opponent's specific defense. Why will this play be successful? It's a macro view of the game that I've always believed was critical to my success as a player.

After position meetings, we break for a walk-through on the field. We eat lunch. After lunch, we do media interviews. Then we have one more team meeting to go though our script and the practice package for that day.

"This is what we are going to run in practice," Coach Hufnagel announces. "Any questions? Make sure you know what's going on."

After that, we have twenty minutes to get dressed and head out to the field for a practice drill. Practice lasts for around two hours. We come back to the locker room, shower, then (except for Fridays) regroup for a forty-minute meeting to watch practice tapes. About four o'clock some guys will take off and go home. Others head to the weight room to lift, and some others stay to watch extra film.

When I was a younger player, I'd always stay and watch film. I remember many times Greg and I would still be at the stadium at six or seven o'clock, bleary eyed, watching game film and falling asleep over it. One of us would wake up with the tape over, the room silent.

"Hey, dude, time to go home."

Even during my off-hours around the apartment, I'd watch game films, or I'd bring my playbook out and study it. I didn't understand the game as much as I do today, and I had more time as well. But as my pro career matured, I stopped bringing my playbook home. I've seen the plays. I get it. I don't have to see it again fifteen times to understand it. My learning curve each week got more and more compressed.

Over the years it became more important to me to spend time with my family than to watch film. I came to see that the relaxed downtime I spent with Ginny, AJ, and Chason actually helped sharpen my game. It's easy to get lost, doing the work and not realizing what it's all for. My family centered me.

In the NFL, families are discouraged from coming along for away games. The good thing is that we're only away from home for a maximum of thirty-six hours. We're not gone for weeks, like the players are in baseball. We always come back immediately after games, and the game-week process starts all over again.

That was the routine, three days in a row, Wednesday, Thursday, Friday. When Sunday rolls around, you put away the diagrams, the film, the playbook, and hit the field, trusting that you know it.

TIKI INTERVIEWS TIKI

Q Do you think you belong in the Hall of Fame?

A It doesn't weigh on me, because it was never my goal. I never said to myself, *I'm playing football to get into the Hall of Fame.* Early in the 2006 season one of our beat reporters wrote that the only player the Giants have had in the last fifteen years who had a chance to make it into the Hall was Michael Strahan. And it's true. Michael will be a Hall of Famer. After that story, reporters started asking me, "Do you think you're going to be a Hall of Famer?" Honestly, I never thought about it. Then a mini-debate ignited, especially after it became public that I was going to retire. I had people telling me, "If you play two more years, or even just another year, and you have a season like this one, you're a shoo-in for the Hall of Fame." One thing football has taught me is to be true to myself. I never played the game just to accumulate stats. I'm not going play because I want to make the Hall. Players should be judged on their body of work, and what I've done over the past seven years speaks for itself. Whether it will get me into the Hall of Fame or not, it's not my call. It's out of my control, so why worry about it? Other factors enter into a player's performance, situations he has no control over. I think of my hero Walter Payton, and compare his early Bears teams with the Dallas Cowboys around Emmitt Smith, for example, where there were Pro Bowlers literally left and right. But the thought of the Hall of Fame only enters my consciousness when someone asks about it. My jersey is already in Canton, from my last game. *Maybe* one day my bust will be there. But if it's not, Ronde's will be. . . .

FOOTBALL ISN'T
EVERYTHING

I want to illustrate what New York City is all about for me, and at the same time provide a glimpse into what happened to make me restless enough to leave football.

March 18, 2004. Ginny and I and several other couples headed out for a celebratory dinner for my son Chason's first birthday. Chason himself had just taken his first tottering steps, but he wasn't exactly an open-field runner quite yet, so he was still too young to bring along. It was an adult dinner to mark a child's birthday.

We went to Tao. It's one of my favorite restaurants in New York, one that, for me, typifies what the elegance and sophistication of Manhattan are all about. It features Asian cuisine, and I love Chilean sea bass on skewers, but all the food is good.

What makes Tao spectacular, though, is the setting. It's on 58th

Street between Park and Madison, a few blocks from our apartment, and it's lodged in a carriage house of the Vanderbilt family, descendents of Cornelius Vanderbilt, one of New York's original multimillionaires. So the place has history behind it.

But the Tao designers gutted the space, filled it with fabulous antiques and objets d'art, and turned it into a cavernous Asian fantasyland. Dominating the space is a huge Buddha. Whenever I go there, I feel as though I am a million miles away from my normal day-to-day environment, which is not bad for a trip of a few blocks.

We had a good time that evening. The two-level restaurant alternated between the raucous and the serene. They seated us right below the Buddha, which is surrounded by a reflecting pool. We were with our friends. Ginny and I were feeling warm and sentimental on the occasion of our second son's first birthday. It was his accomplishment, but we felt like it was ours, too. We sat underneath the giant Buddha statue, talking, laughing, and eating the great food.

Then, mid-appetizer, the whole mood suddenly shifted in the restaurant. A phalanx of large, very serious gentlemen entered, all with those curving earpieces behind their ears that look like prawns.

"Okay," Jay Glazer said, checking them out, "that's somebody."

We knew that some celebrity or dignitary had just descended into the midst of us mere mortals, but we couldn't really see amid the dozen or so bodyguards, associates, and assistants. All we saw was a man in a suit, elegant and elderly.

Whoever it was, his security personnel fanned out through Tao, one in one corner, one in another, yet another posted at the door upstairs. They trolled through the room, walking by the tables, checking each and every one of us out, giving us all a cold-eyed, assessing stare. It was a little spooky. We laughed about it.

"I guess we're safe here tonight," I remarked.

"Anyone with a trench coat comes in, we'll just send him over to that table," Jay cracked.

Later, a person from the table in question, an assistant, approached us.

"Shimon Peres would like to meet you," the assistant said to me.

I had to admit I was taken aback. "Okay," I agreed, rising from the banquette. "Sure."

"At least now we know who it is," Jay said. I could see he was duly impressed.

I caught myself thinking an old, familiar thought as I crossed the floor of the busy restaurant. *I'm just a football player. Why does the number two man in the Israeli government want to meet me?* I had spent my whole life trying to shrug off that phrase—"just a football player"—but I guess I still had some distance to go to lose it entirely.

Shimon Peres. One of the heavyweight movers and shakers on the world stage. Former Israeli prime minister, at the time I met him the vice premier, a man whose history went back to the founding of Israel. When I approached his table, he welcomed me warmly.

"My people tell me you are the best at what you do," he said.

"Thank you, I appreciate it," I said. "It's an honor to meet you."

We spoke for about ten minutes. I could feel not so much a language gap as a cultural gap. They don't play American football in Israel. I was twenty-nine; he had just turned eighty. He made the point that sports and athletics can bring people together. Not an astonishingly original thought, but when the vice premier of Israel says it, you tend to listen.

"You should come visit my country," Peres said.

"That would be great," I replied.

And that was that. Or so I thought. I went back to my dinner. As it was the off-season, I had a lot of speaking engagements and commitments. It wasn't as though I forgot about meeting Peres, but it wasn't at the top of my mind, either.

Somewhere, deep in my psyche, it was probably still that old bugaboo—*I'm only a football player*—rearing its ugly head. As on *Wayne's World*: "We're not worthy! We're not worthy!" I'm not worthy to be a player on such a vast stage as world political affairs. That, at least, was what my unconscious mind may have been telling me.

Then I happened to speak on the phone to a friend, a fellow student in the Commerce program at UVA.

"Libby told me you met Shimon Peres," my friend Rich said. Libby was Rich's wife, an Israeli-born woman who happened to work with Peres. "You're thinking about going over there?"

Well, yes. I was thinking about it. But thinking and doing are two different things. Rich had just returned from what he described as a "life-changing" visit to Israel.

"You should go," he urged me. "You should really take him up on that."

So I did. I called the telephone number that Shimon Peres had given me that night at Tao, and Ginny and I set up a trip for that June, right after mini-camp. The party would be myself and Ginny, Mark Lepselter and his wife Amy, and an NYPD detective named Kenny Cardona, a friend who sometimes provided security for me. Kenny is a detective first grade who became a trustee for Manhattan South's detective endowment association. He also happened to be a friend of Mordecai Dzikansky, an NYPD detective who was posted to Israel as an anti-terrorism investigator.

We showed up at the JFK terminal for El Al, Israel's national airline, the safest carrier in the world. I did not come to realize it until later, but the five of us represented the setup to some sort of joke. We were a black man, an Asian woman, two Jews, and an Italian. We all walk into a bar, and . . .

The El Al security personnel in the screening area took one look at us and started in on the questions.

"What is your business in Israel?" "Why are you going?" "Who are you going to see?"

I couldn't lie. I had to tell the truth. Problem was, the truth sounded outlandish, at least to the security people.

"We're going to see Shimon Peres."

As soon as it was out of my mouth, I could visualize actual alarm bells going off. The effect was immediate.

"Oh, really," said stone-faced security guy number one. "Going to see Shimon Peres?"

They broke us up and questioned us separately to make sure our stories matched. Even though they did, it took Kenny Cardona reaching out to someone who vouched for us to grease the wheels. No one knew who I was. Saying "Tiki Barber of the New York Giants" is essentially meaningless to someone who comes from a country where they don't play American football.

On the flight over, some of the Hasidic passengers got together in prayer groups before takeoff, midflight, and before landing. It sent a certain Old World vibe. But Tel Aviv was an ultimately modern, secular city. Israeli women are among the most beautiful I have ever seen: curly brown hair, blue eyes, olive skin, dynamite bodies.

I couldn't help but be a bit disoriented. *Where am I? Am I in the Middle East? What is this place?*

Our hotel hugged the shore of the blue, blue Mediterranean. Right across the street was the beach. After all the images of violence and bloodshed from the Middle East, I found it difficult to believe that this lovely, resort-style locale was part of it all. I had a distinct impression of this part of the world from watching the news, and my first glimpse of Israel effectively overturned it.

The official reason for our visit was for me to put in appearances at a series of sports schools organized by the Peres Center for Peace. The idea behind the schools is very simple: get Israeli and Palestinian youths together, put them onto a soccer field (or a tennis court, a basketball court, a tae kwon do dojo, etc.), and teach them basic skills—including, most importantly, how to interact with one another in a competitive but nonviolent way.

Peres calls them "Twinned Peace Sport Schools," and they help bridge a cultural and religious gap that is ever-widening. It's probably something that will take generations to even put a dent in, but Shimon Peres is trying, a commendable effort and one that I wanted to get behind. The camps started in 2002, with seventy kids in twice-a-week sessions, once-a-month social events, and mixed Palestinian-Israeli teams playing matches together.

By the time I visited, there were eight of the schools, and we went to all of them. It was a learning experience for both me and the kids involved. I learned that they didn't know anything at all about American football, and they learned that an athletic English-speaking foreigner wasn't going to be able to teach them much about it.

I tried. At one of the first camps I visited, in the Muslim Quarter of the Old City of Jerusalem, one of the kids actually had a football. "Yes, yes," he crowed, trying to dribble it like a soccer ball, "American football!"

We fooled around with it for maybe ten minutes, and a few of the kinds managed to toss an okay spiral. But all in all, it was hopeless.

"Listen," I said to my hosts. "Instead of me trying to teach them football, why don't we have them teach me soccer?"

That was much more successful. Not that they managed to teach me how to dribble a ball with the feet in that fantastic, effortless way that kids have when they grow up with it. But at least we had a lot of laughs. It's a universal equation: children + ball = fun.

Driving through Jerusalem on the way back from the camp, I meditated on the incredible divides common to this part of the world. The Israeli side of the city was green, lush, and modern. It was well-irrigated, with flowers and fruit trees and vegetation. East Jerusalem, the Arab side of the city, had by an accident of geography less rainfall than the Israeli side. It was parched, a desert. Many of the houses crumbled in decay. Like night and day.

History in that part of the world isn't abstract. It's right up there in your face. It's not a course you take in school, it's in the lungfuls of air you breathe wherever you go. This was all the more apparent when—in between visiting sports camps—we toured the holy sites of Jerusalem.

Being there made the hair on the back of my neck stand up. I didn't really care whether I was being archeologically accurate or not: When I went to the Church of the Holy Sepulcher, I felt as though the cobblestones were the same ones walked upon by Jesus and his apostles when they entered Jerusalem. There was a power in the landscape that felt impossible to deny.

A power—and a tragedy, also—because Old Jerusalem was another place where the divisions of the Middle East were brutally apparent. We visited the Wailing Wall, which our guide described as "the first fax machine," since the tradition was to write prayers on tiny slips of paper and insert them into the wall. Those prayers, tradition said, went straight to the ear of God. Immediately adjacent to the Wailing Wall was the Temple Mount, one of the holiest sites for Islam.

Viewed dispassionately, it's an interesting puzzle, how the two peoples live amongst each other and can't find a way to be together. One of the holiest sites for Muslims is a hundred yards from the holiest site for Jews—in my terms, only a football field away. In fact, the Temple Mount is holy to both faiths. They are both "people of the Book," and they share a common heritage in Abraham. They are both Semitic people. And yet they can't abide each other. It's religious and it's cultural and it's socio-economic, and it seems insoluble.

I felt like I was light-years away from Giants Stadium, from my concerns and preoccupations and urgencies. I was restless. My world was shifting, and I couldn't get my footing anymore. I know that people come to Jerusalem from all over world, and it affects them in different ways. Some reinforce their faith. Others spin off into fanaticism. All I knew was that the place was taking me by the nape of the neck and giving me a good shake, just as it had done to a whole lot of other visitors.

I toggled back and forth between the Peres Center for Peace schools, with children modeling how people from different backgrounds can get along, and the grown-up Israeli world. The debate going on back then was all about Ariel Sharon's plan to disengage from the Gaza Strip and parts of the West Bank.

Almost every car had either a yellow or blue flag flying from its aerial, depending on whether the owner was for or against disengagement.

Kenny Cardona was our ace in the hole. Through his direct line to Mordecai Dzikansky, he had inside intel about what was going to happen when. We were headed to a sports school in Sderot, near the Gaza Strip, when Dzikansky called Kenny. He advised us to tell our driver not to take the main highway. Demonstrations. That night on the news we saw Arab protesters tossing oil and nails on the highway on which we would have been driving.

A couple of days into our visit, our group had the official meeting with Shimon Peres. We went to his office in Tel Aviv. I was welcomed as though I were a visiting dignitary. The press corps was there, taking pictures of me and Peres shaking hands, just like they do with President Carter or Bush or whoever is there. We sat on the couch and had a photo-opportunity chat.

I'm thinking, *What the hell am I doing here? Shimon Peres and I are having a discussion?*

He had two people on the other side of him, and two other people on the other side of me, media cameras, reporters looking at us. *Oh my God,* I thought. *What is this? What am I supposed to say?*

But we actually had a good conversation, discussing athletics, the Twinned Peace Sports Schools, and his philosophy about raising kids. It was interesting, but it was bizarre, because (did I need to remind myself?) I'm a football player from Roanoke, Virginia, playing for the New York Giants.

Peres started out his political career as a hawk. He was an associate of David Ben-Gurion, the founder of Israel, and Moshe Dayan, the dashing eye-patch-wearing soldier. Peres was a soldier too, like every Israeli citizen, and he rose in the ranks of government to lead the defense ministry. But later on in life he transformed himself. He founded the Peres Center for Peace.

Hawk into dove. A soldier to a man of peace. He became an example for me, not for his politics (I wasn't going to move to Israel), but as an example of transformation.

Later on, toward the end of our visit, I floated on my back in the Dead Sea, almost 1,400 feet below sea level, rendered ultrabuoyant by the water's 30 percent salt content. I drifted for about an hour. Ginny swam too, and Mark and Amy, but for a while I was alone, suspended in the warm water, closer to the center of the Earth than I have probably ever been.

On our drive down the twisty, mountainous road to the Dead Sea, we had passed Bedouin encampments. The nomads in these tent villages seemed to be living on the edge of nowhere. As I floated, I thought about the vision of those people, those lives I knew nothing about, using camels for transport and tents for housing. I realized how sheltered my comprehension of the world really was.

It's like the lens on a camera. If you focus tight on something, it's hard to realize what you are actually seeing. You see only a fragment. But if you widen it out, you can see the whole landscape. Things become clearer. I realized that this was what the trip to Israel meant for me. It had widened my view of the world.

I knew that in a couple of days I would fly back to the greatest city in the world. I would head to training camp in Albany in August and then play football in the preseason and in the sixteen games that were the real thing and afterward if things went well in the play-offs.

I knew I was going to have a good season, because I was in better shape than I had ever been before and my confidence was never higher. But at that moment my restlessness told me I wanted something more, something else. Football wasn't the only thing, football wasn't everything, football wasn't forever.

Transformation. Football player into . . . what? What did I want to be when I grew up?

Maybe I didn't decide right there, afloat in the salty, overheated bathwater of the Yam ha-Mavet, the "Sea of Death." But the seed had been planted.

TIKI INTERVIEWS TIKI

Q Can you see a future beyond broadcasting? Could there be politics down the line some-where?

A Again, I'd never say never. Right now, I love my job, and I am concentrating on learning my craft and spending time with my family, being there as my sons grow up. Sometimes football seems a million light-years away. But so does running for a political office.

P.S. My wife said she'd divorce me if I ever became a politician.

LOSSES: BOB TISCH AND WELLINGTON MARA

During the 2005 season, I racked up the best numbers of any Giants running back in history. More than that, I had among the best single-season performances of any NFL player in history. I began my professional football career as a roster player, certainly not a superstar. But as of the last three seasons of my time in the NFL, I had stepped up. I had made the transition from good to great.

I don't make this claim to boast, but to look at my experience and understand how I achieved the result that so many people are seeking.

That crucial 2005 season, I had not one but two personal guardians perched on my shoulders. The first was the memory of Wellington Mara. The other was the memory of Bob Tisch, a man I was, in a sense, much closer to than Wellington. Along with Mr. Mara, Bob was the co-owner of the Giants, and in a spooky instance of synchronicity, he passed away within four weeks of Wellington.

The example set by these two men infused my life as a professional football player with meaning. A lot of people don't know why they do what they do. They've lost the motivating reason somehow, somewhere along the line. If you don't know why you are doing something, how can you really excel at it? Conversely, if you can locate meaning in your work, you will inevitably try to perfect your performance.

That's the gift Wellington Mara and, even more so, Bob Tisch gave me as I clawed and fought and scrabbled on my way toward becoming an accomplished running back. They helped me understand that playing football, at its best, could be about much more than moving a ball down a field.

It took a while for me and Bob Tisch to become close. Bob as a team owner was well known around the locker room as a guy who almost comically couldn't remember the names of the players on his team.

He was notorious for not knowing who guys were. Our nameplates were always displayed over the top of our lockers, and Bob would walk in, look up, and say, "Hey, Steve, how are you doing?"

If I had gone and sat in Michael Strahan's locker space, Bob would have walked by, looked up to check the nameplate, and said, "Hiya, Michael." I know this to be true, because several players tried it. LT (Lawrence Taylor) started it soon after Bob purchased 50 percent of the team in 1991. From then on, the nameplate gag became a running joke.

But during my third year on the team, I encountered Bob once when I was nowhere near my locker. I didn't have a jersey on that read "Barber," either. I was just me. And Bob passed by and said, "Hi, Tiki." It actually made my day, I was so pleased that Bob Tisch finally knew who I was.

At that time, I was the only player among the Giants living in the city. I convinced my best buddy on the team, Greg Comella, to move in a year later. Return man Chad Morton eventually chose to take up residence in Manhattan. But most of the New York Giants live in New Jersey.

Because I lived in Manhattan, my relationship with Bob Tisch started to develop and deepen. Bob was a New Yorker. He knew everyone and everybody on the island. Because he knew I lived there, he would introduce us to people, or suggest events to do or see. He became part mentor, part godfather to me and my family.

I remember he asked me to be the emcee for an event honoring a Democratic candidate for a city office.

"Bob, why are you helping organize this?" I asked. "You're a Republican."

"Well," he said, as if stating the obvious, "he's going to win."

Bob was always savvy like that, an affable realist when it came to alliances and friendships.

In a funny way, my life pattern seemed to roll out from a series of seemingly random decisions. Because I loved my wife and I wanted to do something to make her happy, I moved to Manhattan. It didn't have to be that way. I could have taken up residence in New Jersey with the rest of my peers.

But because I became a New Yorker, I had a lot of opportunities that I wouldn't have had otherwise. I became New York City's New York Giant. And because New York is such an incredible center of power, culture, and society, I met numerous people I would never have met if I had retreated to a gated community in Saddle River. I wasn't just an athlete. I was a New York athlete. That gave me a lot of connections in a world that was light-years away from my roots in rural Virginia.

Bob Tisch made it happen. He was my key to the city, an ambassador who enlisted me to become *his* ambassador. He was a real New York City presence, always aware of everything that was going on.

That included what was going on with me. Anything I would do, he would know about. It was uncanny. We were looking for an apartment to purchase, and Bob called us out of the blue.

"I know a realtor I want you to talk to," he said.

How did he know we were looking for a place?

When Ginny became pregnant with our son AJ, Bob's assistant called me. "Bob says to say congratulations."

I called him back. "How did you know?" I asked. "We've barely told our own families!"

"There's not much that goes on in this city that I don't know about," Bob said, Yoda-like. "Especially when it comes to my players."

I was getting schooled in a classic New York phenomenon, an element that has always characterized the place: clout. It's a concept that can get a bad name, but seeing it up close passing through the hands of Bob Tisch, I was fascinated. *This is the way the world works,* I thought, as though I had never really understood it before.

Bob always looked out for us. He enjoyed seeing Ginny and was always asking the two of us to come on board with charity events. He organized a favorite initiative, called "Take the Field." Starting with a poorly maintained high school or middle school athletic field, Take the Field would sweep in and renovate them from top to bottom, installing state-of-the-art facilities.

Take the Field was my first brush with big-time philanthropy. This was good, I decided. This was a cool way to learn about giving back.

When Ginny and I wanted our sons, AJ and Chason, to attend the 92nd Street Y preschool, we realized applying would be a difficult challenge. In the hypercompetitive world of Manhattan, entry into this particular preschool was a top goal. It was widely considered the best one in our Upper East Side neighborhood. The scene outside the school at the end of the day is like no place else on Earth: cars with drivers lined up one after another, two deep, to pick up four-, five-, and six-year-olds, the young scions of Manhattan.

Bob helped us to start cultivating our relationship with the Y. We became a Y family, going to a lot of events there, contributing time and resources to the facility. AJ and Chason wound up attending preschool there and loving it. It's an incredible education. My four-year-old son can speak to me knowledgeably about the painters Jackson Pollock and Monet. And it probably would never have come about if it weren't for my relationship with Bob Tisch.

In October 2004 Bob was diagnosed with inoperable brain cancer. His doctors gave him only three or four months to live, but he made it all the way into the 2005 football season. He died on November 15, 2005.

Bob's memorial service was held in Lincoln Center's Avery Fisher Hall, with a full orchestra. It was that big of a deal. His family had asked me to speak. I didn't write a script. I didn't formulate any remarks. As soon as I entered the hall, though, I was seized with a sudden attack of stage fright.

What have I done? Why haven't I prepared? Here were New York City's movers and shakers, Bob's friends and associates, all those whom he had touched over his incredible lifetime in New York. What could I possibly say to them?

Bob's son Jonathan, now at the helm of the Giants, kept questioning me about my remarks. "We want to get an idea what people's speeches are going to be," he explained.

I had no clue, because Bob meant so much to me, but probably not in the way he meant so much to everyone else. Football wasn't his job, it was his passion. And I was there to represent that.

Even though there were tears on all sides, somehow the mood was upbeat, a celebration of Bob's life rather than mourning his death. As I walked onstage I was still unsure of what I was going to say.

A small voice of clarity spoke out as I went to the microphone to speak a eulogy for Bob Tisch. *Just speak from your heart.* So I did. I talked about sides of Bob that I thought maybe some people didn't know, how funny he was, how much of a prankster he could be. He did so much for me, I said, and so much for so many others.

Then I paused, thinking about my friend, holding him in my heart. I smiled.

"To me, Bob's greatest accomplishment was that he made a country boy from Virginia who moved to New York City feel like I was Jewish."

Laughter rocked the house. It was that kind of memorial, good-hearted and warm.

I lost my good friend. Bob Tisch was the person who—along with my mother, my brother, and my wife—opened the world for me.

When I first joined the NFL, the "he's too small" chorus swelled to a roar. I'd never make it in the big leagues, the sports chatterers said. I was, at best, a Dave Meggett–style back: good for third downs and punt returns. The commentators all but paraphrased Randy Newman: "Short people got no reason to play."

Everyone's got someone telling them they aren't any good, they should hang it up now, they shouldn't even try. We have all had that burden in our lives. It probably has to do with how the naysayers feel about themselves deep down, and they naturally turn their negativity outward.

But what I'm always interested in is how people react when they are told they're too dumb, too little, not good or pretty or strong enough, doomed to fail. In the face of the chorus of negativity, how do we keep keeping on?

I can't speak for anyone else, but I can tell you how I do it. And I think there may be some lessons in my experience, for anyone who wants to apply them, about how to get your head screwed on right to persevere through difficulties and obstacles and the world's unanimous certainty that you're just too damned small to be any good at all.

What you need is one person, beyond yourself, to believe in you. One person to go against the prevailing wisdom and the naysayers. One person to recognize your potential. A mentor. I actually think these people—those who recognize talent and are enthusiastic and encouraging—are as rare as talented people themselves.

For me, Wellington Mara was that singular person. He was the one who recognized and embraced my potential. His coaches might have suggested that the New York Giants draft me, but as owner of the team Wellington Mara had the final say.

And he said yes. His yes was more powerful than all the no's of the naysayers.

Wellington and his brother inherited the Giants from their

father, Tim. Wellington was only fourteen years old when he became co-owner of the team in 1930.

It's an incredible story. Wellington's father, Tim Mara, was a larger-than-life figure, a bookmaker and horse player back before the NFL became all sanitized and corporate. He was there at the beginning, when college ball was the national obsession. No one apart from Tim Mara and a few other visionaries such as Pittsburgh Steelers owner Art Rooney believed professional football could ever be successful.

Wellington had been a ball boy for the Giants since he was eight, and six years later, when his father divested his financial interest in the team, he wound up an owner. His whole life was the New York Giants. Football, family, and God. That was Wellington Mara's trinity.

I knew him. Not well, and mostly through his grandsons, who were ball boys for the team and with whom I had solid relationships. But Wellington Mara was, for me, a symbol of everything that was right with the league. He was always there on the sidelines, propped on a portable cane seat that he carried. And I'm not just talking about every game. He was there for every practice as well. Every time the Giants were together as a team, Wellington Mara was there. No exceptions.

So during the fall of 2005, when he began not showing up, when the cane stool didn't appear and the sidelines got a little emptier, I knew that he was in a bad way.

The last Giants game that Wellington Mara had any consciousness of was our incredible come-from-behind win over the Broncos at Giants Stadium on October 23, 2005. It was a game that the Giants would normally lose, because we were behind in the fourth quarter and the Broncos were a good team. Before that inspired season, we had never been able to come back in those kinds of situations.

Well, we came back.

We won on what was literally the last play of the game, when Eli threw a two-yard touchdown pass to Amani Toomer.

Because we won on Sunday, the team had the day off on the following Monday. That was the traditional reward from the coach for winning, for a job well done. But on this Monday, the fact that I was free gave me a chance to go up and see the ailing Wellington. His family called me and asked me to visit.

So I saw him one last time before he passed away, to say thank you and to pay my respects to a great man.

He had given me my chance. Even though there was a chorus of people chattering about the fact that I was too small to make it in the big leagues, that I wouldn't amount to much, that the Giants shouldn't waste a draft choice on five-nine Tiki Barber from UVA, Wellington Mara believed in me.

I might have been one of Wellington's favorites precisely because I bucked the odds. I wasn't always good, but I always played hard, and Wellington was the kind of man who respected that.

That Monday afternoon just before he died, I wound up being one of the last players to see him. Me and Jeremy Shockey. Shockey was another Wellington favorite, the only contemporary player who had the stones to call Wellington by his old nickname, "Duke."

The tag had started when he was still a kid, and his father's friends jokingly named him "Duke" after the Duke of Wellington, but as he aged into a gray eminence, nobody else dared call him that to his face. Apart from Jeremy, who always just naturally dares when others don't.

I went through the whole week thinking about Wellington. In the early 1960s, he and his brother Jack had a decision to make. They could share television revenues with smaller market cities like Green Bay and St. Louis, or they could keep the fat New York receipts to themselves. They decided to share. That single decision turned out to be crucial to the survival of the NFL. Wellington's loyalty to the league was greater than his self-interest.

I attended Wellington Mara's funeral that Friday at St. Patrick's Cathedral on Fifth Avenue. It was a crisp, cold, overcast morning. It sounds strange to say, but this is the only way I can express it: It was a perfect day for a funeral. Like one you would see in the movies, with everyone wearing black on an autumn morning.

I wound up on the first bus with all the coaches on it. I sat somewhere up front. When we got to St. Patrick's, I just happened to be the first person off the bus, so I wound up leading the team up the wide stone steps into the cathedral.

John Mara, Wellington's oldest son, who is now running the Giants, gave the perfect eulogy. It had some humor and some sentiment, and John really captured who his father was. If you had never known Wellington, this eulogy would tell you what you needed to know. When it was over, and despite the formality of the occasion, all of us wanted to applaud. I think some us actually did.

We had practice later that day, after the funeral, because Coach Coughlin wanted us to. We got onto the buses and drove back over to Giants Stadium. It was still a gray day, but just as we headed out and started stretching, the sun broke through the clouds. A beam of light shone down directly on our practice field.

Coach Coughlin happened to be walking past me when it happened.

"Hey, Coach," I said, pointing to the sky. "That's Wellington, looking down on us."

Tom squinted upward. "Yeah, you're probably right," he replied.

Certain days defy all logic. The Sunday after Wellington Mara passed away was one of those. It had become invested with profound emotion for me. So it was definitely not "any given Sunday," as the phrase goes, but a very meaningful one.

October 30, 2005. At Giants Stadium, we faced the Washington Redskins. Playing the Skins was always special for me, because I grew up in Virginia and Washington was the NFL franchise nearest to me. From the earliest time I remember, I was a Washington Redskins fan. You never entirely lose the allegiance you have for the team you rooted for as a boy.

But because of Wellington's death, this game had the weight of added meaning. Against the Redskins that day, I had a ridiculous game on the field. Energized and inspired by the emotional memory of the elderly man who loved his team so much he never missed a practice, I began by breaking off a fifty-nine-yard run on our first play from scrimmage. It went on from there. By the time the third quarter rolled around, I had piled up just over 200 yards rushing.

But I didn't have a touchdown. I kept getting tackled before I could cross the goal line. Brandon Jacobs banged it in after I powered a drive deep into Redskins territory, or Shockey grabbed a TD pass, or Jay Feely would kick a field goal. So I had lots of yardage, and we were winning, but I hadn't scored yet.

Tim McDonnell, Wellington Mara's grandson and one of the

ball boys with whom I had become close over the years, walked by on the sidelines and joked with me as the fourth quarter started.

"Hey, Tiki," he said, "are you going to keep getting caught or are you going to score me a touchdown?"

I smiled and joked back. "I promise you I'll do it for your grandfather."

On the first series of the third quarter, on a draw play from the Redskin four yard line, I made good on that promise.

I blew a kiss to the stands, grabbed the ball, and delivered it into the hands of Timmy McDonnell.

"This is for you—this is for your family," I told him. "I love you and I love everything you guys have done for me."

Then I went to the coach and took myself out of the game. This was a privilege I had been granted as a Giants veteran, to judge for myself when I was too beat up to play. I was emotionally done. I had fulfilled my promise to Tim and, in a larger sense, to the memory of Wellington Mara.

From that point on, the season became my way of thanking Wellington's family for the kind of organization that they tried to run. An NFL franchise is a business, and a business can be run in a lot of different ways. Wellington Mara and his family operated the franchise with character, class, dignity, and excellence. It wasn't a faceless corporate monolith. It was a heroic human endeavor.

It became a driving motivation for me, to honor the Wellington Mara tradition. I tried to become a torchbearer for the team. When things got tough, it helped me snap back into focus and push through.

2005 was that kind of season. Triumph in the face of sadness and adversity. My experience that year capped my football career. Once a struggling and middle-of-the-pack player, I rose to the top of the NFL heap.

That Sunday against the Redskins, I had one of the top games of my career, 203 yards over three quarters before I took myself out. We blew the Skins away, 36–0. Tim McDonnell still has that game ball, which he displays in his office.

Football, family, and God.

"Penultimate" is a word a lot of people mistakenly use to mean "ultimate ultimate," or "more ultimate than ultimate," but all it really means is second to last. But in my case, my penultimate season, in 2005, was also my "ultimate ultimate" season.

I put up record-book numbers. Given the storm of controversy my retirement announcement made in 2006—it was front-page sports-section news for ten days straight—I know I probably shouldn't say it, but in a lot of respects 2005 was my true last season. As LT once told me, "I quit in '91 but retired in '93."

I had traveled a long way to be inspired by old-school Irish Catholic Wellington Mara and Jewish New Yorker Bob Tisch, unlikely mentors for a small-town kid from Virginia. When I started out at point A, I had no idea it would lead me, years later, to point B. But good people I met along the way made all the difference.

The motivational boost I got from honoring the memory of Wellington Mara and Bob Tisch carried all through the 2005 season. My teammates were on fire, especially Plaxico, Shockey, and Eli. The offensive line's fierce blocking opened gaping holes for me to power through.

Apart from the late team owners, other influences were in the mix too. For overall determination and competitive spirit, I could reach all the way back to growing up under Geraldine's watchful gaze. I tried to emulate her determination and grit. My wife and children provided a foundation of love and support to remind me why I tried to be the best at what I did.

Greg Comella's example continued to motivate me even after he left football and went on to Harvard Business School. I got plenty of "utils" (utility) from Joe Carini's strength training, and more from the "I can do it" mentality his training fostered. I still carried with me the essential training and instruction given to me by former coaches and teachers, from George Welsh and Sean Payton. Friends such as Mark Lepselter contributed camaraderie to the equation.

Ronde and I met long distance every week on *The Barber Shop*, our show on Sirius Satellite Radio. We talked football, of course, but we also talked music, current events, whatever was on our minds that day. It was as though listeners were privy to a phone conversation between the two of us. Most importantly, the show provided a weekly connection to my brother. Talking with Ronde always helped to ground me.

The inspiration of all these people worked to make 2005 my most effective season as a running back. I could not have done it alone. Multiple factors and circumstances conspired, but most of all, it was people.

In the last regular-season game of 2005, on New Year's Eve at Oakland, we were still jockeying for postseason play-off position, so it was a game we needed to win. With eight minutes left in the first quarter, we were backed up on our own five yard line with second down and fifteen.

We broke huddle and went into formation. The wide receiver

was in tight, so he could get in and block the safety. The fullback was "strong"—meaning we were in a strong set and Finny was crossed over. He was not directly behind Eli in the "I"; he was positioned to the strong side.

A pure power-running formation. Sometimes we might run play-action out of this set, but given the situation—backed up on the five yard line—we couldn't risk an interception on a play-action.

The result was that every savvy person in the stadium knew what was coming, including the Raiders defense. Their safety began running down, cheating toward the line of scrimmage to stop the rush. Eli might not have even seen him, but it didn't matter, because this was a play you could run into any defense. The optimum result was an eight- or ten-yard gain, but the play was really designed to get three to four.

If one safety came down, the wide receiver would block him. If the other safety came down, he would be out of the play on the far back side.

As Eli was going through his cadence, I saw the linebackers pointing at me.

"Power!" they were screaming. "Power!" Meaning a power run.

Then Oakland's second safety made his move toward scrimmage, and I realized they were trying to push us up against the goal line even more. Their defensive play-callers were rightly convinced that we were going to run the ball. So they made a reasonable decision: Let's blitz off the back side. See if we can clog up the run.

But there was an unintended consequence to that call: It opened a gaping hole in the secondary. With the safeties creeping up toward the line, no one was at home in the middle. It allowed us to push on the back side, because they had committed their safety.

Eli handed off to me just as I crossed the goal line, still five yards behind the line of scrimmage.

With the defensive ends blitzing, the only defenders in position to stop me were the linebackers. A quick note on an arcane bit of football terminology: Because there are eleven players on a football team, and eleven is an odd number, football formations are usually asymmetrical. One side is weighted heavier with players than the other. The side with more players—usually an extra wide receiver—is called the strong side. The side that's shortchanged is called the weak side.

Let me introduce you to three of my nemeses: Will, Sam, and Mike. They're pretty amazing guys, since they play on every team in the NFL. They are the weak-side linebacker (the "Will"), the strong-side linebacker (the "Sam"), and the middle linebacker (the "Mike").

On this play, Finny would be blocking the Sam. David Diehl, our guard, was pulling—meaning he would come off the line and move laterally to help with the blocking. He was my key. A lot of linebackers watch the guards like birds of prey eying a rabbit. If the guard pulls, the linebacker goes that way too. It was knee-jerk automatic.

I knew that the Mike and the Will would follow Diehl, and Finny was taking care of the Sam. So I changed direction, cutting that gaping, ragged hole in the middle of the line. I powered through untouched. Oakland's free safety, Stuart Schweigert, a quick, six-foot bruiser, tried to scramble back into position, but he couldn't reach me in time. I brushed past him at the fifteen.

That left the Raiders cornerback, Nnamdi Asomugha. I jitterbug-faked, and Plaxico laid a block on Asomugha. Plax turned around after dispensing with the cornerback and once again accompanied me, bodyguard-style, down the sidelines to the end zone.

They put it up on the JumboTron. A new Giants record for a run from scrimmage: ninety-five yards. Besting Hap Moran's ninety-one-yard mark set way back in 1930.

Everything clicked that season. It was the Giants' twenty-first NFC East championship, which pulled us ahead of Green Bay as having the most division titles in the league.

Everything clicked, but nothing seemed to negate the persistent restlessness I felt. The sound of thousands of fans chanting "Tiki!" at Giants Stadium didn't drown out that small inner voice saying, *Time to move on.*

Part of it was our ignominious postseason collapse just a week after the record-setting triumph against the Raiders. Our first and only play-off game that year was a shutout loss to the Carolina Panthers at home on January 8, 2006. Five turnovers, zero points. A totally deflating finish to a totally incredible season.

I had high hopes going into the game, but there were ominous signs that I could have read if I would have allowed myself. The Panthers defense was ranked fourth in the league, excellent against stuffing the run. This was essentially the Super Bowl XXXVIII team we were facing. Heading them up as coach was a familiar face, John Fox, who had been the Giants defensive coordinator in 2000.

Fox had been one of the prime architects of our Super Bowl year and the defensive genius behind the Giants' 41–0 shellacking of the Minnesota Vikings in the conference championship that season. He was canny and resourceful, and he knew our team well. A formidable adversary.

I didn't think it mattered. We were 11–5 and had grabbed the division title. Carolina came to us as the wild card. I had ultimate confidence that my storybook season would continue into the play-offs and help us snag the Lombardi Trophy.

"Hey, Elisha," I said to Eli Manning when we got ready to go out onto the field. Whenever I wanted to get his attention and maybe goad him a little I used his full given name. "What are we going to do today?"

"Why, we're going to win, Teek," Eli answered, in his usual flat-calm way.

It didn't happen. I knew something was wrong right away. I got the call on five of the first eight plays, all runs, and got pretty much stuffed at the line every time. I'd accept the ball smoothly from Eli, look for the crease, and then bang against a mash-up of linemen and linebackers: jaw-jarring defensive ends Julius Peppers and Mike Rucker, defensive tackles Brent Buckner and Jordan Carstens.

I couldn't understand it. I was being stopped for one-yard, two-yard gains every time. As I scanned their defensive set, I realized they were flooding people into the box, meaning they were bringing up their linebackers to the line and cheating up their defensive backs. Between the tackles was like Times Square at rush hour.

Still, the Giants kept giving me the ball. I had a touch on the first play of five of our first six possessions. The Panthers were keying off me. They knew I was coming, and they slammed the door shut again and again.

It was frustrating, but at the same time I knew that if we just kept banging away, I would break something open. Some off-tackle runs ought to loosen up the box a little, spread the formation so I could find running room. Open field was where I prospered. Downhill into the throat against these guys? It just wasn't working.

We made stupid mistakes. At times the ball literally did not bounce our way. Late in the second quarter, we were behind only by a touchdown, even though we had been pretty much spinning our wheels on offense. Then a punt took a squirrelly bounce and hit the leg of Gibril Wilson, streaking up the right sideline with his back to the play. Bad luck, and the Panthers capitalized with a field goal. We went in at the half to a chorus of boos, down 10–0.

I was a little shocked by those boos. Fans can turn on a dime. I felt like I hadn't banked any good feeling for my career year. We had a lousy first half. But one touchdown and we'd be right back in it.

That touchdown never came. The number of blown assignments multiplied. Our play-calling shifted. I began to get fewer touches. I ended the game with a miserable forty-one yards on thirteen carries. That represented the whole of our rushing attack. A running team like we are can't win without a ground attack. The final score was 23–0. We had been shut out for the first time in a decade, and shut out in a play-off game for the first time in twenty years.

Panthers head coach John Fox had somehow gotten right into our huddle. He seemed to know what we were doing before we did it.

The locker room after the game had the stink of defeat all over it. I let my frustration get the best of me.

"I don't think they were more physical than anyone else we played," I told the reporters who crowded around my locker. "I just think they had a good scheme. I think in some ways we were outcoached."

There it was. The *O* word. The press took it and galloped off with it. The newspapers and sports shows were filled with it the next day.

In a sense, it was a calculated comment on my part. The Carolina game was Eli Manning's first play-off test, and it did not go well for him. He threw four interceptions. I realized that as a young player he was going to take a lot of flak, and I felt for him. I knew he could develop into a great quarterback. But if I could step in and take some of the media heat off him at this early stage in his career, it might help him retain his confidence.

But the comment got me into deep water with my head coach. I was upset with Tom Coughlin anyway, since at the same post-game session with reporters, he'd talked about what a "good season" the Giants had—not an opinion I was ready to hear after a 23–0 drubbing.

The next morning at Giants Stadium, as I was cleaning out my locker and saying good-bye to what was, for me, still an incredible season, Tom Coughlin summoned me into his office.

I would say it was like getting called into the principal's office, but I never actually did get called into the principal's office when I was in school, so I don't know what that's like. All I know is that Tom Coughlin was stony-faced when I entered his inner sanctum. But that was all right too, since Tom Coughlin was pretty much always stony-faced.

He was less emotional than he had been the night before. He motioned toward a chair. "Sit down," he said. "I want to show you something."

He had the film of the game all cued up. He scrolled through a dozen plays one after another, and I saw what the coach himself had seen from the sidelines. A Giants parade of missed blocks, blown assignments, broken plays. It was ugly.

After my session with Coach Coughlin, I dutifully went out and modified my remarks to the reporters who were hanging around Giants Stadium for the season postmortem. They clamored for comment, scenting that blood might have been spilled in my meeting with Coach. I still used an O word, but I chose a different one.

"We were 'out-everythinged' by Carolina," I told the press.

Relations were fine between me and Tom Coughlin, I assured the media, who were itching to know what had transpired during our face-to-face. We had "a frank exchange of views," as they say in diplomatic circles.

Still, the Carolina debacle ended my best season ever on a low note. It was like playing a whole symphony and then getting the last chord wrong, or like winning a bundle at a casino and slamming your hand in the door on the way out.

I didn't want a humiliating play-off blowout to be my last game in the NFL. But I felt some of my fire dying down. Getting schooled by Tom Coughlin wasn't a big factor in how I was feeling, but it didn't help, either. As far as I was concerned, whether I would ever come back to another season at Giants Stadium was up in the air.

TIKI INTERVIEWS TIKI

Q What's your relationship with the Giants organization now?

A On a personal level, I have a great relationship with everyone in the organization, from the front office on down. Professionally, I was tired of mediocrity. Because I'm a strong-willed person, and don't hesitate to speak my mind, by the end of last year they were as tired of me as I was of them. I have a lot of affection for the people in the Giants organization. It will always be my team. But to some degree, I have perspective on the franchise now. The Giants need to do a much better job selecting talent in both the college draft and the free-agent market in order to build a foundation for winning. It's worthwhile paying a premium for top players; however, the problem for the Giants is that over the years there have been a number of guys making big money and undeservedly so. I was always cognizant that my undying loyalty to the franchise probably cost me millions of dollars over the course of my career. Compared with other top running backs in the league, for example, you could argue I was underpaid. I understand that this is a business. I was putting up numbers comparable to those of all of the top running backs in the league, and most of them were earning significantly more than I was; in some cases twice as much. I don't hold a grudge, but that is a fact. I take responsibility for signing the contracts and agreeing to the terms.

LAST SEASON:
PART ONE

I recall lying on a couch in my apartment in January 2006, feeling restless and weighing reasons to stay or go, to leave football or commit to the Giants for another year.

I had a massive bruise on my right thigh, a hematoma, and when I rubbed my hand across it I could feel the effused blood squish under the skin. Okay, so I'd had plenty of nicks before in the game. But the ones I got during the 2005 season just underscored what I was feeling overall.

I'm getting too old for this. I was only thirty-one, young by most standards, but geriatric for NFL backs. Careers of pro running backs average 2.5 years, less than the league's overall 3.8-year average career. That's because running backs are football's crash-test dummies. They take a beating that ranks right up there with the ones taken by middle linebackers.

My heart wasn't in it. Somewhere along the line—maybe in those two face-offs in his office—I lost my connection with Tom Coughlin.

In my first years in the NFL, I came up with Jim Fassel and Sean Payton. They were both creative, intuitive guys. Somehow, they made us feel we were all involved in an exciting enterprise, everybody in it together. There was strength in camaraderie.

Coughlin's style was much different. He was a strict disciplinarian. He directed everyone through the same drills, veterans or rookies, nicked or not. That method might have been okay for college, or for the younger pro players, who had to be told to arrive at a meeting five minutes beforehand, but it wasn't a good fit for me.

My heart wasn't in it. That's a key phrase right there. The previous year, playing to honor Wellington Mara and Bob Tisch helped me understand why I was doing what I was doing. It helped me put my heart into it, helped me to have an elite-level season.

My agitation and desire for change stemmed from more than any one game, more than the aches and pains that took me longer to recover from each year. I wanted to leave the game upright, not hobbling. Every time I put on the pads, I faced the possibility of a debilitating injury.

It's a complex dynamic, America's attitude toward its sports stars. An ice-cold current runs beneath all the warmth. Some sector of the public, or some part of the human psyche, takes pleasure in seeing idols tumble. A has-been superstar—there's something perverse to relish there.

"How the mighty have fallen." We all love to be able to say those words. "He went out on top" is always high praise, but there's disappointment couched in it too. How could he deprive us of our moment to mock him?

Let's shake the pedestal, see if the hero falls off.

I saw that sensibility in the reaction to Jerry Rice's final years in the league. Jerry Rice is one of the game's all-time greats. Yet as he stayed on after his glory years, his play diminished. He left an image of himself that wasn't right. I detected a smugness in the public reaction to that. America has a love-hate relationship with its heroes.

I considered leaving after 2005. I discussed retiring with Ronde, Ginny, and Mark Lepselter, as well as a lot of other people. I didn't exactly keep it a secret. I could go back to the 2006 off-season and point to numerous times that particular sentiment—"I'm thinking of retiring"—leaked out to the press. But for a long time I held off on a definitive public decision.

I'm getting old and I've got other things that I'm excited to do. So why not leave now? I wanted to go out with class and panache and dignity. What better moment than after the kind of year I had in 2005?

On the other hand . . . well, the other hand didn't have a Super Bowl ring on it. That's the snarky joke I've heard folks tell about me and Ronde: "They're identical, except for one thing. Ronde has the ring." When Tampa Bay won it all in San Diego at Super Bowl XXXVII at the end of the 2002 season, I was genuinely happy for my brother. I kept any twinge of competition in check.

But I still wanted a ring of my own. I honestly felt positive about our chances to win the Super Bowl in 2006. Given the year the Giants had in 2005, the next season promised to be even better. The veteran core of the team would be back again.

In the end, the possibility of going out on the very tip-top—of retiring with a Super Bowl ring—won out over my restlessness, and my aches and pains. I decided to play for one more year.

I played in 2006 because I thought my team, the New York Giants, was talented enough to go all the way. That was my reason, and it was a good reason, but as it turned out it wasn't reason enough.

The fields of the NFL represent some of the most exclusive areas on the face of the planet. It's like the holiest of holies. Within the perimeter, only twenty-two players (plus seven officials) are allowed entry at a given time. And only those twenty-two can truly understand what happens there, what it feels like to step out onto that field.

Or off of it.

The football field resembles the center of the bull's-eye. The coaches and personnel on the sidelines know a lot about what's going on in the bull's-eye, but even they are outside it. The journalists in the press box at Giants Stadium know a lot too, and the fans who come out for the games. The television audience gets a pruned-back, carefully controlled vision of the action, but dedicated followers of the sport can understand quite a bit from watching it on TV.

No one experiences the game like those twenty-two guys. That's just the way it is. You can pretend to understand, you can fake understanding, you can talk as though you understand everything, but in the end you're just speculating. Even the knowledge of former players fades. The only ones who really know are the ones in the bull's-eye.

I was back inside the bull's-eye for the 2006 season. I could better gauge my performance than anyone else—coaches, fans, or reporters. The hits at training camp seemed tougher to take. The preseason appeared to stretch longer and be even more irrelevant than it used to be. As soon as the regular season began, I second-guessed my decision to play for another year.

I was still putting up good numbers. Four games into the season, I was the top rusher in the league. I remained in the top five for the whole year. On the surface, everything was fine. From the perspective of the coaches and Giants personnel on the sidelines, I was having another stellar season. Even my teammates, wrapped up in their own concerns, probably didn't notice anything wrong or different.

But I knew. I had plenty of touches that year. My knowledge of the game hadn't changed; in fact, it had probably increased. The blocking was still phenomenal. But I soon realized that I no longer had the skills to do everything I needed to do as effectively as I needed to do it. I had lost a step.

What once could have been a fifty-yard run, that year resolved itself instead into a twenty-yarder. I could still achieve at a high level, and the view from outside the bull's-eye looked pretty good. But my personal judgment of my own performance was ruthless. I felt like a swimmer in a pool where the plug had been pulled. I was still doing my laps, but I could feel a subtle underwater tug.

How much did I miss that lost step? I was sickened by it. If I am not getting better at what I do, I feel like a failure. I've been that way ever since I was a kid. Progressing, stepping up, is what it's all about for me. So to feel myself slipping that year, however imperceptible the effect was to other people, made me certain the time had come to go.

Coming off the four-game preseason in 2006, the Giants' prospects looked good. I hadn't played at all during our preseason opener in Baltimore but had some touches against both Kansas

City at home and against the Jets—also at home in Giants Stadium, even though we were officially the "away" team. For our final preseason game against New England, I played hardly at all.

For me, preseason was a waste. A lot of veterans feel this way. For younger guys who are struggling to make the team, it's a vital test. Rookies are all pumped up about it, just as I was in my first season. Preseason or not, there's no feeling in the world like stepping out onto a game-day NFL playing field for the first time. You've made it into the bull's-eye.

Ten years in, everything was different. I was fearful of being injured and ruining what I knew was going to be my last year. I've never been a big fan of preseason, because as a running back it doesn't do much for my learning curve. Other guys need to get hit, they need to get their timing with the quarterback, or work their defensive schemes. But in my job, specifically, I'm not going to get a lot out of playing the preseason.

Whenever I did get sent into a preseason game, I flashed back to when I pulled my hamstring against the Jets in 2001. Beneath the ministrations of Dr. Rob, I healed quickly, but the injury had a huge impact on my game. That was the only year in the last seven in which I did not have 1,000 yards rushing, and the last time I didn't play in all sixteen regular season games.

I know the annual Jets-Giants preseason matchup is a hugely popular tradition, a battle for neighborhood boasting rights. But I had gotten burned by it once before. I actually felt as though the game might be jinxed for me. I didn't want to get hurt for nothing again. But I made it through the preseason that year unscathed, and the Giants emerged from it unbeaten.

Four games, four wins. So far, so good.

September 10, 2006. We opened the regular season with a high-profile Sunday night game. NBC debuted its new show, *Football Night in America*. Sportswriters dubbed the contest the "Manning Bowl," because Eli faced off against his brother Peyton and the Indianapolis Colts. It was the first time in NFL history that siblings would start as quarterbacks on opposing teams.

All the Manning Bowl hype just annoyed Eli. I guess at one time, when he first saw the schedule, he may have found it mildly interesting that he would face his brother, but by the time the game rolled around, he was already sick of the whole concept. He never really brought it up. He just didn't care. We loved that about Eli.

The pressure must have been murderous to deal with, being compared to the best quarterback in the game right now, and maybe the best of all time. As much as the Manning face-off was a source of discussion outside our locker room, inside it meant absolutely nothing. Which was a good thing.

The home crowd booed when Peyton was introduced. They cheered for Eli. Peyton had an excellent first half. We kept making dumb mistakes. A missed field goal. A couple of dropped interceptions that would have been drive-killers for the Colts, but wound up as simple incomplete passes. Suddenly it was 13–0, Indianapolis.

Then Eli led one of the prettiest drives of the season, a deft eighty-six-yarder that featured a couple of eleven-yard rushes by yours truly, as well as a seventeen-yard pass reception. We were cooking.

Eli hit my man Plaxico with a thirty-six-yard touchdown strike to finish the drive. Nobody does an aerial dogfight like Plax. He tangled with cornerback Nick Harper three feet off the ground and came down with a stupendous catch.

When our defense was out on the field, I watched Peyton

Manning from the bench. Both Mannings are good, but Peyton is older, and a few more steps down the road than Eli. He's smart. He understands the game thoroughly. Peyton's wife Ashley was at business school with my brother and me.

"All Peyton does during the season is sit in front of tapes and study the opposing team," she told me.

He's one of the best quarterbacks in the NFL, maybe one of the best of all time, and yet all he did was study. Perhaps that's what makes him the best. So on game day, when you make that one little mistake, he's got you. He catches it. You probably don't even know when you mess up. He knows.

The Colts like to take the entire play clock on offense. Peyton effectively runs the huddle from the line, in position behind the center, so that the opposing team can't substitute defensively. He freezes the defense. It's a stingingly effective way to run an offense, but not many teams—and not many quarterbacks—can manage it.

Watching from the sidelines, I could gauge how much Peyton's use of the so-called "muddle huddle" represented a calculated psychological gambit. It was unnerving to see him standing there behind the center, repeatedly stepping forward or back, turning around for calls or play adjustments or to survey the defense.

We all have our psychs. I can get my ass beat, get banged around and hit hard. But I always get up with a smile. Inside I may be pissed off. But you'll always see me smile. That's my psychological advantage. If someone hits me hard, I get right up. "Good hit," I say. "I'll see you next time."

Everybody asks me, "Why do you always smile? You just got *blasted*." Why would I give an opponent the satisfaction of knowing that he'd just hurt me? When I get up smiling, he might say to himself, "I gotta hit him harder next time." But if he consciously tries to hit me harder, he's more likely to mess up. As soon as he loses his level of control, he becomes vulnerable.

Peyton Manning is master of the psych, master of control.

His brother Eli is not there yet. Eli's young, and it takes a while to mature as a quarterback. Go back and check out the early seasons of Super Bowl MVPs such as Terry Bradshaw or Brett Favre. Eli's already a good quarterback. Whether he becomes a great one depends on if he can step up.

He did his best to do so that evening, with his family and half the country watching. During the second half he had a fumble and an interception, both just after we had closed to within two points, and both of which led to Indianapolis scores. But the Manning Bowl (unlike the game itself) came out as a draw. Eli pretty much matched his brother stroke for stroke.

For me, that night marked the game during which second-year Giants halfback Brandon Jacobs fully came into his own as a short-yardage, goal-line bulldozer. In the fourth quarter, with the score standing at 23–14 in favor of the Colts, I had contributed thirty-nine combined yards to a drive that brought the ball to the fourteen of Indianapolis.

Whenever we had penetrated deep into an opponent's territory like that, the call went out for Jacobs. I'd liked Brandon immediately when I met him the year before, his rookie season. A powerful runner who had been raised in Louisiana football country, Jacobs did well in 2005 and was looking to build on that in 2006.

I stood on the sidelines and watched Brandon do his thing. An end run to the right side for eight yards. Between the tackles for five. First and goal, one yard line.

Short yardage goal-line plays represent the bread-and-butter of football. If you can't have a near-perfect record with them, you'll go hungry. I did the job for a long time. I was able to be effective at it because I could get lost. I would hide behind my lineman, find a little crease, and explode into it. I'd either get into the end zone directly, or draw the defenders and then bounce outside of them, running for the corner.

On goal-line stands, the defense was compressed into limited territory. So the secondary could not necessarily key on me, because they would be in so tight. If they were in normal open-field formation, ten yards deep, they would be able to see the play develop more clearly. The closer they got to the line of scrimmage, the more obscured their view. Near the goal line, I could hide a little bit and spring free.

That's important, because short-and-goal there's always going to be one opponent unblocked. You either have to trick him, as I would do, dipping and ducking, or you have to run his ass over.

That was Brandon's way. A lot of times it's more effective to have a back who will say, "Fuck it, I'll run right through him."

Which is what Brandon proceeded to do in that instance against the Colts, a pile-driver run off right tackle for the one-yard touchdown. It was the start of a string of short-yardage touchdowns for him, during which he went twelve-for-twelve. Like I said, you want to be perfect once you get that close.

The drive brought us again within reach of the Colts, 23–21. Two points. A field goal would put us in the lead. There were eight minutes left in the game, which was plenty of time.

But we let it slip away. The defense stopped Indy and we got the ball back. At third and two on our eighteen, Eli lofted a great pass to Tim Carter along the right sidelines for an eighteen-yard gain. But the back judge called Tim for offensive pass interference. Part of being a good football player is learning to take what the officials dish out, good, bad, or ugly. But this one was hard to take.

On the next play, Eli threw a soft pass over the middle for Amani that was taken in by the Colts' Nick Harper. Seven clock-eating plays later, Indianapolis's Adam Vinatieri kicked a field goal, putting the Colts ahead by five, 26–21. In the minute left in the game, we tried for a score, but came up short.

So the Manning Bowl was a draw, and the game itself was very close. We played the best team in football down to the wire. We had opportunities to win. We felt like we should have won. We ran the ball very effectively, with a good per-carry average. Brandon had ten yards per carry, and I had upwards of six.

After the game, Eli exhibited the same outward calm as he always did. Eli had the same emotion after every single game. He never changed, never deviated. That's his blessing and his curse. It can cut both ways.

The Colts game turned on the fact that we just couldn't make a stop defensively. Football is all about momentum. All we needed was one or two stops, maybe one, and the momentum would have stayed with us rather than going back and forth. We had the chance of knocking our opponents out. But time and time again, the knockout punch never got delivered.

The next Sunday at Philadelphia, the Eagles were the team that couldn't deliver the knockout.

It was so hot that day that exerting myself on the field made me feel as though I was dying. We were all sweating to the point of dehydration. We were constantly on the sidelines, sucking down fluids. Later in the game the temperature turned cooler, so we began to function better.

Going into the game, I felt my usual single-focus mentality, even though the week before I had made a crucial move in my career. Lep and I had told both of the media outlets for which I worked back then, Fox News and Sirius Satellite Radio, that I would be retiring at the end of the season. I wanted to clear the air and give sufficient notice about my change of status. But I put those discussions out of my mind as we faced the division-rival Eagles.

We started out pretty well and made a little discovery about Philadelphia's pass coverage early on. The secondary played in to protect against the rush. A football field is a closed system. When they cheated up to stop the run, they opened themselves up for the pass. That's how my rushing and the rest of our ground game worked to help free up our receivers.

Amani recognized the gaps in the Eagles' scheme and just kept running for the end zone. Eli finally connected with him for the first score.

Then Philadelphia just took over. The Eagles played a hurry-up offense, which in the heat wore out our defense. We were just gassed. They methodically moved the ball down the field and scored a touchdown.

Again and again, our drives stalled out because we couldn't get our running game established. The Eagles defense was guessing, keying on a lot of our schemes, and guessing right. I had a horrible day: seventeen yards rushing in regulation play. The heat beat the crap out of me. Philadelphia controlled our ground game, which is our strength. We weren't completing any passes. We'd give the ball back to them and they would always do the same thing. No-huddle, seven- or eight-minute drives down the field, bam-slamma-bam. It wore our defense out.

The Eagles scored twenty-four unanswered points after that first touchdown of ours.

Four minutes into the fourth quarter, I turned to Eli on the sidelines. "You know what? Let's just try to score a touchdown," I said. "Let's try to make this look respectable. Because it's going to be 31–7 before long, for chrissakes. It's going to look ugly."

I was afraid that after our good feeling from week one, we would start to feel worthless, starting the season off with an 0–2 record.

The Eagles got a little bit complacent. Defensive tackle Jon Runyan was joking around and he got a stupid penalty. It didn't have any direct effect on the game, but he got flagged for offensive holding. Somehow, though, it was indicative of what was to happen.

We got the ball back with 3:59 left in the third quarter, down 24–7. The air was cooler now, and the humidity was less oppressive. For the first time in the game we were able to move the ball. Eli made a pass across the middle to Plaxico. In trying to break a tackle, Plax fumbled the ball forward. Tim Carter made a great play by knocking Philly's Michael Lewis out of the way to fall on the ball in the end zone.

The fumble-touchdown that day was one of those unbelievable miracles that happen only because a football is not round and sometimes refuses to bounce in predictable directions. Because the ball squirts off *there* instead of *here*, all of a sudden a light breaks through where before there was total darkness.

"All right," I said to Eli on the sidelines, as we were standing there a little dazed by our good luck. "We're back in it a little, I guess. We still have ten points to go."

After trading series, Philadelphia got the ball and was moving it down the field. Eagles running back Brian Westbrook tried to jump over a pileup at the line. Free safety Will Demps recovered Westbrook's fumble.

As the Giants offense went into the huddle, we all had the same thought. "Hey, we're in a great field position," I said. "We could really do this."

That huddle was the last in the series. We tore a page from the Eagles' playbook and went no-huddle ourselves. Philly's defense appeared blown out and confused. Even then, still ten points down, I had the thought: *We've got them.* The momentum had swung around to us.

Eli threw a pinpoint strike to Amani at the back of the end zone. Nobody in the league gets his feet down like Amani Toomer does. He's so aware of where he is on the field and where his body is. He caught Eli's pass in the end zone, gave two quick touches to the turf with his feet, and now it's 24–21 with five minutes left in the game.

"Oh, fuck, we can win this!" Shockey screamed into my face on the sidelines. We just needed one stop from our defense, which we got with just under a minute to play.

The Giants offense took to the field once again, and we drove from our twenty to our thirty-eight. But with thirty-eight seconds left in the game, a pass play looked as though it was going to be broken up. I was blocking for Eli, who was under pressure and about to get tackled. Nobody was open. But Tim Carter broke to his right, and Eli lofted the ball into the middle of the field, over the linebackers and in front of the secondary.

Carter came down with it. It was a great play. Eli picked himself up, rushed forward, and spiked the ball. We moved forward ten more yards before Jay Feely kicked a tiny field goal to tie the game with ten seconds left.

Sudden death. One of the great, terrifying phrases of football. In overtime, I felt certain that we were going to win the game. We moved methodically down the field. For the first time all day, we ran the ball effectively and nailed some first downs.

Understandably, Philly got desperate. The Eagles were seeing a game that they had firmly in hand slip away. All they could do was all-out blitz us. But the pass rush freed up our receivers to go one-on-one with Philadelphia's defensive secondary. The first time they blitzed, we missed the opportunity. But the second time they did it, Plaxico found himself running into single coverage again.

The pass coverage may have been man-to-man, but every receiver on the team had been running sprints for about an hour. They were all cramping up. Amani and Tim Carter came off the line of scrimmage on what was to be the last play of the game, but they both seized up with cramps and collapsed to the ground. The play broke up. Philly had us.

Except for Plaxico. The blitz was so confusing that I couldn't figure out who to block. I was just standing there in the backfield, exhausted, when the Eagle Sam pounded in toward Eli. I reached up and barely got my hands on him. But it was enough so that Eli could come off his back foot and fling the ball down the middle of the field.

Plaxico was one-on-one with a lone defender. The football was up for grabs. Plax leaped, caught the ball on the one yard line, and fell forward into the end zone. We won the game, 30–24.

Normally, with a game-winning score, every Giant on the team would be screaming, but we were too spent. This had to be the most feeble game celebration ever. Plaxico staggered to his feet after the catch and tried to throw the ball all the way out of the stadium. He could only make it halfway up into the crowd.

After Eli threw the touchdown pass, I just stood there, so tired that I couldn't even cheer. I saw Plax make the catch, but I could barely register my jubilation. Thoroughly exhausted, I walked like a zombie over to Eli.

"Hell of a job, man," I said. Because it was Eli, really, who had won that game for us. Then I walked off the field. I didn't celebrate. I had no energy left.

TIKI INTERVIEWS TIKI

Q You retired at the top of your game. Doesn't a pro athlete have some responsibility to the fans?

A Of course, and I think I fulfilled that responsibility pretty well. I think every one of my teammates, and everybody who ever watched me play, knows I always gave it my all, and that will be my legacy. I know a lot of fans feel ownership toward the athletes on their team, but that's just a delusion. No one owns the decisions I make for myself and my family except me.

RETIREMENT
CONTROVERSY

It's an up-and-down ride, the NFL. Every week over the course of the season, you see the same pattern with team after team. Highs and lows, hills and troughs. We came out of Philly feeling we had pulled one out of the fire.

We were lucky to win in Philadelphia. It would have been extremely hard to overcome an 0–2 start because of the difficulty of our schedule. Going into Seattle with two losses and facing the defending NFC champions would have been daunting. Very rarely do East Coast teams win those jet-lagged games, especially against what had been the best team in the conference the season before.

So even though we had lost game one, after the amazing win in Philadelphia, we still felt we had upward momentum. But as it turned out, the New York Giants never showed up in Seattle. Our charter plane must have been lost in the Bermuda Triangle somewhere, because the team sure wasn't on the field that Sunday.

It was pitiful. It was worse than the first half of the Philly game. Plaxico had nicked himself against the Eagles and didn't practice all week. The hero of the previous Sunday had a tough game that day. He had a fumble and dropped a deep pass. Coach Coughlin benched him in the third quarter. Ups and downs, hills and troughs.

Seattle scored twenty-one unanswered points in the first quarter. We kept fighting for the whole game, but it just wasn't enough. Our incredible twenty-seven-point "comeback" in the fourth was the proverbial too little too late. Final score: 42–30.

It was disheartening, especially because we'd had a very emotional win the week before. In some ways the Philly win may even have harmed us, making us feel that no matter how deep a hole we dug, we could always force a fumble, or cause an interception, and recover to win the game.

"Every time you lose," said George Allen, "you die inside, and every time you win, you're reborn."

The flight back after a blowout loss was always an hour-by-hour process of forgetting. The closer you got to home, the farther away you were from the pain of losing. On the way back from Seattle, I sat in the cockpit.

The Giants had an early bye in 2006, in week four. We used it to lick our wounds. In position meetings, I talked about playing to our strengths.

"We have to run the ball," I said to Kevin Gilbride, the QB coach, and John Hufnagel, the offensive coordinator. "We need to make sure we get twenty carries every game."

I thought it was obvious that we weren't running the ball enough. Was this just my running-back perspective? Not necessarily. The Giants have always been a great running team. We're good at it and we've always been good at it.

"I know we have talented wide receivers," I said to Huff. "But this is a running conference. If we don't start to develop it we'll be in trouble."

It's not as though we had been ineffectual on the ground. We had a great average. So we put an emphasis on it the week after the bye in a game against the Redskins. We didn't do anything spectacular. We drove the clock and made the plays when we had to.

That's football. Football is about field position, which means you control the ball and you don't turn it over. The ground game was a reliable part of that very basic strategy. We climbed back to .500 at home against Washington, winning 19–3.

Then we played Atlanta, which was another good team from the year before. The Falcons have Michael Vick, an obviously lethal offensive weapon, and they have a highly touted defense. According to the media leading up to this game, it was obvious that the Giants didn't have a chance running the ball against such a fearsome D.

I heard a couple of sportscasters whom I respect say much the same thing: "Don't expect a lot out of Tiki this week."

A game such as this one becomes a battle of which team can run the ball the best. We thought this was going to be one of those days. The Falcons had played Tampa two weeks before and rushed them for 340 yards. Ronde told me about it after that game, and it didn't sound pretty. Everyone was saying Atlanta's running game was going to take them all the way to the Super Bowl.

October 15, 2006, at Atlanta's Georgia Dome. What had been lost on the sports commentators for the previous two years and even so far in 2006 was that the Giants have a pretty damn good running game. And against Atlanta, we finally got to it. We began clipping off fifteen-yard runs, twenty-yard runs, eight-yard runs.

That didn't happen until the second half. During the first half, Eli threw a few interceptions. I talked to Huff on the sidelines.

"What do we always say?" I asked him, repeating what had been my mantra. "If we're not producing the pass, just hand it off. It'll be okay. I promise you I'll get you four yards at least."

The theme presents itself over and over again. When all was said and done we beat the Falcons with our running game. We beat them at their own strength. I ran for 185 yards. We had a total of 239 rushing yards. We dominated the clock, 34:18 to 25:42, so we didn't give them a chance to do what they do best.

The issue would come to a head later in the season, when Tom Coughlin and I got into a minor dustup over it. But it's not as though all of a sudden I got pissed off that we didn't run the ball. It was a continual thing with me. I always sounded the same note. We have to run the ball, because we are a running team. I am, not to be brash, one of the best running backs in the NFL. Why am I not being used? Let's use me.

We employed the running game against the Falcons, and— *boom!*—it proved my point. We beat a team on the road that people didn't think we could beat, by rushing for 239 yards. We hit full stride as a running offense.

Why does the importance of a running game get lost? Because it's not sexy. A four-yard run does nothing for the viewing audience. You'll never see an offensive coordinator who runs the ball forty times a game be touted as a head coaching candidate.

Pro football is a field-position game. It's not about scoring every time; it's about moving the ball consistently and controlling the clock so that the other team doesn't have the ball. It's about pinning the opposing team in a bad field position, making a defensive stop—which means that you get the ball again. Then you move downfield again, controlling the clock to get closer to scoring.

That day in Atlanta, we ran the same two running plays over and over. In essence, I guess, it was actually four plays, because we ran them to either side. It was always "Thirty-Six Boss," which was an inside-outside read. I'd follow the fullback, Finny, and his responsibility would be the safety. If the defensive end ran upfield we'd run inside at the end. Finny would block whoever had the bad luck to get in his way and I'd just keep going. It was so simple.

We alternated Thirty-Six Boss with a stretch play to the side. Football is not rocket science. Football is cake. You find your advantage, which is not hard to do, and then you exploit it. Over and over again. And then, when they figure how to stop it, go to the other side—until they figure that out. On defense, get the ball into the hands of your teammates. That's it.

My utilitarian philosophy of football was grounded in my business training. In business school, one of the professors went up to the chalkboard on the first day of class and wrote "KISS."

Keep It Simple, Stupid.

I even did the same thing one time in a position meeting at Giants Stadium. I wrote "KISS" up on the board. Do what you do best until they stop you. If they stop you, then you worry about it. If they don't stop you, don't worry about it!

Motivational guru Marcus Buckingham had a basic message:

Play to your strengths. Buckingham's book *Go* was centered on how most people, when they want to improve, talk primarily about their weaknesses.

In the case of the Giants, what do we do poorly? We don't throw the ball consistently very well. All right, let's spend most of our time on the passing game to make it better.

Forget about the fact that the Giants have been one of the top rushing teams in the league for the last couple of years, and that we have one of the best per-carry averages over the last ten. No, let's focus instead on what we do poorly.

Buckingham said that a weakness-based approach was exactly ass backwards. Focus on your strengths. Your weaknesses will pull themselves up if your strengths continue to empower the rest of the package.

In the days after the Atlanta game, my own strengths and weaknesses would be put on display for the whole world to see. It began with a children's book, and it didn't end until I was publicly flogged for daring to claim that I had a life of my own.

Sports and commercial aircraft flights might be the last authoritarian realms left in America outside of the military. Don't do exactly what the flight attendant tells you, and the air marshals will meet you at the gate when you land. Speak up if you're on the active roster of a sports team, and the commentators raise a howl.

After week six of the 2006 season, we looked pretty good. Following losses to Indianapolis and Seattle, and wins against Philadelphia, Washington, and Atlanta, we were 3–2—not ideal, but well-positioned enough to be competitive in the crucible of the NFL, where parity was everything and not many teams were coming through their seasons unscathed. Within our division, Philly was 4–2, Dallas 3–2, and Washington 2–4.

In mid-October, *New York Times* reporter John Branch "embedded" himself with Ronde and me for a day or two as we promoted our latest children's book. Branch followed us around New York to signings and public appearances. As he listened in on my conversations with my brother, he picked up on the obvious. This year was going to be my last year in the NFL. I was going to retire.

I didn't make any formal announcement to Branch. It's just that we didn't hide the truth from him. Ronde would make a comment, and I would respond.

The issue finally came to a head during a photo shoot for *People* magazine, in a studio near my apartment on the Upper East Side. Ronde and I were being profiled in the magazine's annual "Sexiest Man Alive" issue. George Clooney took the honors again that year (he had made the grade once before, in 1997). But Ronde and I were featured, along with the tennis double team of Bob and Mike Bryan, as "the sexiest twins." Silly, but fun.

Branch, still tagging along with us throughout the day, approached me. We had made an agreement with him that what we said during that day was off the record would not be reported in the *Times*. But my retirement seemed to be a gray area for him.

"Am I hearing this right?" he asked. "Are you going to retire this year?"

"I'm leaning toward it," I said.

Branch was quiet for a moment, absorbing the news. "Your mind's made up?"

"Pretty much," I admitted.

Again, a short silence as Branch digested the news. He looked like a young cat who had caught a mouse and didn't know what to do with it.

"Is there anything that would make you reconsider?" he asked.

"Nothing," I stated.

As I said out loud to a reporter what I had been saying privately in my mind and to my friends (and what I had referred to repeatedly before in other contexts, though never with such finality), I realized once again the degree of certainty I possessed about the matter.

I was leaving football.

My long love affair with a game, a passion that had begun on the forty-yard off-tackle touchdown run with the Cave Spring Knights, had come to an end fifteen years after it began. There were manifold reasons, including aches, pains, and a hematoma on my leg the size of a whoopee cushion.

But let me say it clearly: Much of it had to do with Tom Coughlin. He robbed me of what had been one of the most important things I had in my life, which was the joy I felt playing football. I had lost that. He had taken it away.

I have to give Coach Coughlin credit. I put up better numbers under his coaching than I ever did before. He helped me in my effort to hold on to the ball and hold down the number of times I fumbled. All that said, he just wasn't a good coach for me.

Even though I had all these feelings roiling around inside, I didn't reveal them to John Branch that day. We proceeded through our schedule of appearances, signing a lot of books for kids and their parents. Ronde and I had a good time together, as we always do. I didn't feel as though I had dropped the "R-bomb"—about my retirement—in any significant way.

Branch took me aside as his time with us ended. "Tiki, I feel conflicted," he said to me. "I feel as though I have a news story here, and I don't know if you want me to print it."

I hemmed and hawed and finally told him to go ahead. I was naive. I didn't think it would be a big deal. As I indicated, I had been talking retirement for months, years even.

Later that day, October 17, the *New York Times* posted Branch's story on its website. A lot of people have the *Times*'s online news alerts sent straight to their computers. The effect was instantaneous. The chat rooms, sports websites, and blogosphere began to hum with chatter.

Lep and I were out at Rosa Mexicano, a favorite restaurant of mine, when we got a call from Peter John-Baptiste, the Giants PR director.

I was nursing my favorite drink, a top-shelf tequila, but Peter sounded real sober and serious on the phone. "This is going to be huge," he informed me. "Get ready."

"Oh, shit," said Lep, much more upset than I was. Maybe the tequila was working its magic, but I still didn't feel a media fuss was something I couldn't handle.

"Don't worry," I told Lep. "It will all blow over."

The resulting story kicked off a ten-day media blitz, the biggest news cycle of my career. The ins and outs of my retirement and my personal life were splashed front-page on the sports sections for more than a week.

The coverage didn't exactly consist of tributes to my career, either. It was overwhelmingly negative. One theme: I was a "distraction" to my teammates. I was labeled self-centered, a loose cannon, not a team player.

Much of the coverage sounded the theme of me and my big mouth. Stories dredged up any shred of past history. Here were my sins, according to the sportswriters:

"To some extent we were outcoached." (About the 2005 play-off loss to Carolina)

"No." (In answer to John Branch's question, "Can anything change your mind about retiring?")

The first one was judged as a challenge to the dictatorial supremacy of Giants head coach Tom Coughlin. And the last one, well, that was just an insult to the gods of football.

The *Times* ran a good paragraph with online comments from fans, wittily correlating their sentiments with the well-known seven stages of grief, originally formulated by the writer Elisabeth Kübler-Ross:

There was shock ("I am not ready to say good-bye to Tiki"); denial ("Not worried. I don't see him following through on that"); bargaining ("We gotta start a petition—don't do it, Tiki"); anger ("I love Tiki, but does he have to say this now?"); depression ("Now I'm going to cry myself to sleep"); and acceptance ("Only one thing to do now—win the Super Bowl so he goes out on top").

The fans normally only see me suited up on Sunday. They never witness the agony of Monday morning, or all the muscle-straining workouts, the practices, the blood, sweat, and tears it takes to walk out onto the field. They don't see the pain, so they can't believe anyone would want to give up the gain.

For those fans to whom football was a religion, I was a heretic.

For those to whom it was a war, I was a deserter. But that was all just delusional crap. I was neither. I was a human being trying to live his life. Thankfully, I possess this God-given attribute that luckily we all share, which is free will.

I felt a little more cynical about the sportswriters who pandered to this "heretic/deserter" viewpoint than I did toward the fans who believed it. The media fussed over the issue obsessively.

Okay, everybody. Time to get a life.

Mark Lepselter had his own theory of why the press liked to jump down my throat.

"It's envy," he told me. "It has to be. They know that you can you do their job, and that on your best day maybe you can probably do their job better than they can do it themselves. You could be a better commentator or journalist or reporter than they are. But on their best, unimaginably perfect, ultimate day in their lives they could never, ever do what you can do on the football field. So they're screwed both ways. They get envious. It's simple. It explains it all."

I wasn't sure if it was true, but it made me laugh. It still had the power to offend me, though, that "shut up and play ball" mentality. Mike Lupica of the *Daily News* led the charge on that front.

To be an effective player, Lupica wrote about me, means "he shuts up. . . . Barber shuts up about his future plans and he shuts up about his hurt feelings toward people in the media."

The "shut up" mentality represented a throwback to a time when respect for authority was practically a cult. The bosses know best, the government knows best, the powers-that-be know best. Just shut up, little man. It's all a tad undemocratic, isn't it?

Worse, the "shut up" mentality also pandered to that segment of the public who got upset when they saw a black man speaking out.

Yeah, we still live in a time and a world where that kind of reaction is all too prevalent.

A few journalists understand this dynamic.

"It is more than a little distressing," wrote Wallace Matthews in *New York Newsday*, "that here in the twenty-first century, too many of us still have a plantation mentality when it comes to our professional athletes. Too many of us want ballplayers, even the best and brightest of them, to say nothing more than 'yes, sir,' and 'no, sir.'"

Kudos to Wally. My vocabulary is just a little broader than "yes" and "no."

I used some of my vocabulary after our next game, ripping into a media guy. Right in the middle of the Tiki Retirement Media Road Show, my teammates and I headed to Texas to play our division rivals, the Dallas Cowboys.

Distracted though we were (at least, according to the sports commentators), the Dallas game represented a pure team effort. A Monday night game, which meant a national audience. Facing former Giants coach Bill Parcells.

It was also, in a way, the peak of the 2006 season. Over the course of that game and the previous week, we lost four key guys, including Osi Umenyiora, LaVar Arrington, and Amani Toomer. Amani actually tore his ACL the previous week against Atlanta, but played the whole game. Shortly thereafter Michael Strahan got hurt and was going to be on the PUP list for a while.

In Dallas our defense had to make some big-time stops. They harassed starting QB Drew Bledsoe so badly that he began to have problems getting rid of the ball. Parcells removed Bledsoe from the game, sending in Tony Romo for the second half. The Giants defense kept up their part of the team effort, finishing with six sacks and four interceptions. We won the game convincingly, 36–22.

With the win at Dallas, we were on a three-game winning streak, with a record of 4–2. I was leading the league in yards from scrimmage. We were playing football as well as the Giants had all season, going on the road for two consecutive weeks and beating two good teams.

All of this was done against the background noise of sportswriters claiming that with my retirement controversy, the team's chemistry was all messed up. Former Dallas star and ESPN commentator Michael Irvin complained that I "wasn't a leader anymore" and accused me of quitting on my team. I was frustrated and hurt. How could the league's leading rusher possibly be accused of quitting on his team?

So I'd had it up to here with the whole mess. A *Daily News* columnist named Gary Myers came into the locker room after the Dallas game. He hung around my locker and wouldn't leave. Myers asked me an innocuous question.

"Gary, respectfully, I'm not talking to you right now," I told him.

"Why?"

"I have an issue with a story you wrote, because it was asinine."

Myers was one of the columnists who proclaimed how much of a distraction I was to my teammates. But to reach this groundbreaking conclusion, he had not bothered to speak to a single one of my teammates. He didn't ask any of my coaches.

His sources, he claimed, were anonymous. He also claimed that, via my retirement talk, I was posturing for the networks. My football career was over, so in order to make myself attractive as a media personality, I needed to pump up the hype. Then he contradicted himself and said that I was trying to manipulate the Giants into giving me more money.

None of it made any sense. Myers had failed to complete his due diligence. Mark Lepselter and I had spoken to the networks weeks before. Network executives knew about my retirement at the beginning of the season, before anybody else knew.

One person Myers did talk to was Mark Lepselter, who painstakingly explained to him the sequence of events that had led to my retirement becoming front-page news. Lep's words were wasted. Myers played it the way that he wanted to, ripping into me.

"I respect your right to write whatever you want to write," I told him. "But you have to respect my right to tell you that what you write is full of shit."

Myers just wouldn't leave, so I kept on railing at him. It had to be embarrassing for him, because this went down in front of his sports-reporter peers. On some level, though, he must have taken some masochistic enjoyment from the encounter, because he simply stayed there and took it, a sickly half smile spread across his face.

But I couldn't win. The next Friday the *Daily News* ran a full-page caricature of me on its back cover, showing me boxing with Gary Myers.

TIKI INTERVIEWS TIKI

Q You say in this book that Tom Coughlin "robbed" you of the joy you had playing football. Didn't you have your best years under Coughlin?

A Coach Coughlin and his staff helped me immeasurably in becoming an elite running back. At the same time, under his coaching I lost my passion for the game. It's a double-edged sword, because as much as Coach Coughlin helped me, I also helped Tom Coughlin. I can't go into the minds of the Giants owners and say this for sure, but winning the game against the Redskins in 2006 allowed Coach Coughlin to keep his job, because we made the play-offs. I had a career game that day. So you could say that Tom Coughlin helped me learn how to hold on to the football, and I returned the favor by saving Tom Coughlin's job. The hardest thing for me, and one of the reasons I walked away, was that after loving the game for so long, by the end of the last season I resented it.

LAST SEASON: PART TWO

The Barber Bowl.

The Sunday after the Dallas win, on October 29, 2006, we played at home against Ronde and the Tampa Bay Buccaneers. The face-off wasn't hyped like the Manning Bowl was, but Ronde and I didn't really care about what kind of press coverage we were getting. At that point, I was media sick.

Personally we cared, though, because it was the last time Ronde and I were going to play each other. The adventure we had embarked upon more than a decade and a half before was coming to a close. We had a ton of family at the game.

It was not a pretty day for football. There were times during my career when Giants Stadium was not a football field, it was a wind tunnel, and this was one of them. Gale-force gusts blew off the Atlantic and swirled in the big bowl of the arena. The weather became a big factor in the game.

Because of the winds, we couldn't throw the ball. All we could do was run. Our offense, which had been on a roll against Washington, Atlanta, and Dallas, didn't really do anything that day. Tampa stacked the line of scrimmage with bodies because they knew the winds had effectively removed the forward pass from our offensive arsenal.

So the Tampa game turned into a punters' duel. Which, like a pitchers' duel in baseball, can be interesting in a theoretical sort of way, primarily for those fans initiated into the subtleties of the game. For everyone else, it can be deadly boring.

For the team it was almost an uneventful game. For me it was extremely satisfying. I was loving it because my brother was on the field. Ronde tackled me once. He missed me a couple of times. On one play, he grabbed me, had me in his grasp, but then just kind of slid off.

"See?" I said to him as I headed back to the huddle. "I don't go down that easy." I won the head-to-head battle this time. The last time we faced off, three years prior to this game, Ronde had gotten me pretty good.

Early on, I was tackled and went down in a pileup. As I got up, the Bucs defensive end, Dewayne White, put his knee in my chest. After I was finally allowed to get to my feet, I turned to him.

"What the fuck are you doing?" I said. I went over to my brother. "Will you tell your boy Dewayne over there that he's got issues?"

"Yeah," Ronde said. "Don't mess with him. Don't say anything to him, because it'll just get worse."

Gouging, punching, finger-twisting, cleat-mashing—it all goes on, out of sight in the pileup. Sometimes it takes four or five seconds to unpile. The play is over, a half ton or so of human flesh is lying on top of you, and some guy takes the opportunity to jab your neck with his elbow. It happens all the time. It gets lost because no one ever sees it.

Eagles linebacker-prankster Jeremiah Trotter (he also played for the Redskins) once tried to tickle me as we waited at the bottom of the pileup. I can hear those football cynics now: so *that's* what they're doing in those pileups—tickling each other!

Ronde and I always tried to keep it loose around the game. One of the best things in my life was doing the weekly satellite radio show during the season with my brother. It kept us connected, and we had a lot of fun doing it. The talk wasn't always about football.

Ronde: Welcome to the second hour of *The Barber Shop*.

Tiki: That would be the top of the second hour.

Ronde: Why are you busting my balls on this?

Tiki: My bad, dude. Just to let you know that you're on notice.

Ronde: Okay, let's get this straight. Zero-zero is the top of the hour.

Tiki: Yes. Three-zero is the bottom of the hour. Like the bottom of the circle?

Ronde: Oh, I get it! The clock! But you know, I have all digital.

Tiki: Oh.

Ronde: I'm looking at a digital clock in front of me. So how do I know if it's the bottom of the hour? How do I know the big hand is pointing straight down?

Tiki: I thought that was something they might teach you if you watch *Fox and Friends* [a show I was on back then].

Ronde: Shameless plug. Good job, dude, way to go.

Most of the time, we were more centered on football. Ronde was more into setting up the subjects, exhaustively researching the games. He was the knowledgeable play-by-play announcer, I was just the color.

Ronde: Let's talk about the quarterback issues plaguing the NFL.

Tiki: You've got three listed there. Let's start with the first one, Jake Delhomme. No issue.

Ronde: I don't think there's an issue.

Tiki: No issue. Let's put it this way. In my opinion, Jake gives them the best opportunity to win football games. People across Carolina have been calling for his head for two weeks, because he's thrown some inopportune interceptions. I think back to the Cincinnati game, in week nine or ten. . . .

Ronde: About a month ago.

Tiki: He threw an interception in the end zone that could possibly have given them a tying score in that game. Look at this week. And though it wasn't really a bad interception like the one in Cincinnati, it's another bad pass. So [head coach] John Fox is sitting here having to answer questions about his quarterback and whether Chris Weinke is the guy. Obviously, I don't think so. I think Jake Delhomme is a great quarterback. I think he's working with a somewhat average football team right now in a lot of regards.

Ronde: They have a lot of good players. Probably one of the greatest players is Steve Smith. But Delhomme is struggling.

He is making some inopportune plays at bad times in football games. So the question comes up, should he be on the bench?

Tiki: But you know what, there's a lot of continuity that comes with having a quarterback in there. And when he's not egregiously bad—and he's not, because he played good for most of the game—but when it came down to the wire, he made some bad mistakes, and it ultimately cost him. As was painfully obvious. John Fox did not have to answer questions at nearly the rate that Lovey Smith did about Rex Grossman.

That kind of stuff, two hours a week, my brother and I talking about football, music, clocks, cars—anything that stirs our fancy. Mostly football. I wanted it to be as though the listeners were wire-tapped into a phone call between me in New York and Ronde in Tampa. Most of the time, that's the way it worked out.

As the Giants hit a 2006 midseason skid, losing four straight, the sports commentators were really ramping up on Eli. "He's not his brother," was the kindest comment Manning was getting from the press. I got fed up with it and decided to change the terms of the discussion.

I understand how sportswriting works. I've faced reporters since high school. I take pains to learn their names. I try to understand what they need to do their jobs effectively. I can tell if they have already written the story, for example, and just need a few quotes to plug into it. I talk to reporters in a way that a peer would talk to them, as people. I try to avoid sports-speak clichés.

At the same time, I see media interplay for what it is: a huge, meaningless chess game. Meaningless because the only thing that really matters in the NFL is the Ws and Ls. I'm not averse to using the media, just like I'm not averse to them using me.

"A disproportionate amount of teams that win, win it by running the football," I said to reporters after our week-eleven loss to Jacksonville. "Period. That's football. It's not complicated. This is something that teams and kids and coaches do from twelve years old to college and up and beyond. This isn't rocket science. It's football."

All true enough, but my words sent Tom Coughlin right through the roof. He perceived my comments as second-guessing his game plan. We had it out in a shouting match in Tom's office, which no doubt was overheard by my teammates (but not, thankfully, by reporters, who had already left).

"You have a problem, we sort it out among ourselves," Coughlin yelled at me, livid. "You don't go to the press with it!"

I came right back at him. "We just got our asses beat!"

We were both angry, shell-shocked, and disgusted at our collapse.

I believed everything I said to the reporters. But once again, my words were deliberately chosen. I knew how much the press relished piling on me, ever since I used the fatal word "outcoached" in describing the reasons for our 2005 playoff loss to the Panthers, and especially since the retirement storm.

One more studied, ready-made "controversial" comment from me might again take the relentless media spotlight off of Eli, giving him some breathing room, and it worked out exactly that way. For the next week or so, the sports pages were all about me "mouthing off" and criticizing the Giants' play-calling.

"Jive Tiki," read one Thanksgiving headline. I now had yet another speaking-out sin against my name, according to the commentators and columnists.

The howling got louder, of course, because we were losing. Sins are forgiven a winner, but a losing team gets condemned over and over. Fans and reporters alike react to blood in the water.

The turning point of the season had come the week before Jacksonville, when we hosted Chicago at home. Tom Coughlin made the boneheaded call of attempting a long, fifty-two-yard field goal in wind and rain. Jay Feely, our placekicker, was solid from forty-five and in. He'd had an infamous game in Seattle in 2005, missing three field goals, two in overtime, for which he wound up getting parodied by Dane Cook on *Saturday Night Live*.

Against Chicago that night, Feely's kick fell short. Waiting eight yards deep in the end zone was Devin Hester, the most dangerous return man in the league.

When the kick missed, the Giants on the field reacted as though the play was over. Nobody pounded down on Hester. He hesitated, then rocketed into a blazing 108-yard touchdown return, tearing along the right sideline untouched. That run broke our backs in the game, and to some extent changed the course of the entire season.

After that, Jacksonville and another loss. A stunning game in Tennessee, when the Titans did to us what we had done to the Eagles earlier in the season, stealing a game out from under our noses with a big comeback. We led 21–0 in the second quarter, but we couldn't put it away against the brilliant Vince Young and his teammates. Dallas then beat us at home. We were reeling, staggering through the season weak and wounded.

Wounded. Out of all the ink spilled and all the hot air expended on the collapse of our 2006 season, the single word really necessary was "injuries." Amani Toomer, Michael Strahan, and Luke Petitgout were the key losses, but too many Giants were playing nicked. I sprained my thumb during the Chicago game. The locker room resembled a triage area.

Even though we won the game and won a lot of games after it, I always trace the decline of the 2006 season to the first meeting with the Cowboys, in week seven in October. People will point back and say, that was at the height of Tiki's retirement distraction. Actually, the reason we started losing after that was we didn't have any fucking players on the field. Our stars were sitting on the bench, most of them out for the season. You can't win when that is the case. It had nothing to do with me.

Attrition is always as much a part of the game as the forward pass and the open-field run. Oftentimes, the last team standing at the end of the season is the one with the fewest key injuries. Of course, to fill the newspapers, magazines, and airwaves, that one word, "injuries," won't suffice, even though it explains a lot.

Attrition is hard to make interesting. "Key injuries started in the Dallas game, and that's when the season started to fall apart"—that line doesn't supply much of a narrative. "Tiki distracted his team-mates with all his retirement talk, and that's when the season started to fall apart." *That* supplies a narrative.

Reporters and fans like to portray the locker room as a festering soap opera. The truth is that for a majority of players, the game is a job, not much different from a gig at Microsoft or IBM. Many times a player comes into training camp, says hello to his team-mates, and might not say another word to the majority of them that doesn't have to do with football for the rest of the season.

You have a small corps of the guys you run with, have a beer with, and hang out with. Those are the guys with whom you have personal interactions. Everybody else has got their own lives going on. They could care less about the personal decisions of me or anyone else on the team.

December 30, 2006. The last game of the 2006 regular season. A Saturday night game on the NFL Network, at Washington's (actually Landover, Maryland's) FedEx Field. After a 6–2 start, we had spun out in November and December, and we needed this game to hit .500 and, more importantly, sneak into the play-offs as an NFC wild card.

Subplots piled upon subplots. Apart from the play-off possibilities, there was the fact that we were playing near my home state of Virginia, with all that personal history coming into play. If we lost, this would be my last game in a Giants uniform, unless you counted the Pro Bowl, coming up in Hawaii a week after the Super Bowl.

Leading up to the game, the Washington media relentlessly beat the dead horse of my retirement. They said I had lost either my inner fire or my outer focus. I no longer brought my playbook home. I had cashed it in. One rag delighted in referring to me as the "little tailback."

The Sunday before, I played my last game in Giants Stadium. The franchise did it up fine: I was the only Giants player introduced that day, and the fans roared their approval. I had AJ and Chason out on the field with me for the coin toss.

But the coin toss was the high point of the game. The fans booed the team during our 30–7 debacle against my old friend Sean Payton's New Orleans Saints. The game represented quite a send-off from a place that had been my home for the whole of my professional career. I wanted to wipe away the bitter disappointment. I felt for our fans; we played miserably.

In an attempt to reverse the Giants' skid (and probably save his job), Coach Coughlin transferred the play-calling duties for the Washington game from the offensive coordinator, John Hufnagel, to quarterback coach Kevin Gilbride. Coughlin had been captain of the ship for some of the most ignominious losses in Giants history. If we ended the up-and-down 2006 season on a losing note, there was a likely chance the Giants would look elsewhere for a new head coach.

We faced a must-win game with a depleted roster. Toomer and Shockey were out injured. Our offensive line would be playing nicked.

For all those reasons, I felt good when I began ripping off big yardage. Just under two minutes into the second quarter, I found a crease off the left side and busted through for a fifteen-yard gain and a touchdown. We never trailed again. I scored a second time on the next drive, on a fifty-five-yard run with Plaxico providing downfield blocking once again. Twelve carries, 137 yards, and two touchdowns in the first half.

The second touchdown, a fifty-five-yarder, came when I made an off-the-cuff, on-the-field adjustment to our blocking assignments. We'd tried the play, a short-yardage off the left guard, once before, and got stuffed. I saw a possibility for daylight, only to have Finny drop away.

"What happened?" I asked him.

"I was just doing my assignment," he told me. As the fullback, Finny had been assigned a specific player to block.

"Next time," I said, "don't do your assignment. Come along with me."

This was a form of football heresy. If the coaches on the sideline had heard me, they would have went berserk. But Finny wasn't about to rat me out, and I wasn't going to announce my intentions either. I simply saw a way to break the play open.

The next time the coaches sent in the play, Finny and I were ready. We punched through the line on the left, and instead of peeling off, Finny rumbled into the linebackers and the secondary, clearing my way. He sprung me loose, and I was off for my second score of the day, surviving a potentially lethal goal-line hog tackle from Redskins safety Sean Taylor.

That's the way the whole game went. In the fourth quarter, Gilbride called my number on five straight plays on a drive downfield, which I capped with another touchdown run, this one for fifty yards.

Neither the Washington press nor the New York commentators could argue with the numbers. Three rushing TDs, a career-high 234 rushing yards, and 258 all-purpose yards. That's how I always answered whatever was being said about me. On the field. After a nail-biting last few minutes, wherein Washington mounted a two-touchdown comeback try, we won the game, 34–28.

No, football wasn't forever. I didn't even leave it behind that day, since I played in our wild-card loss to the Eagles the next week, and in the Pro Bowl after that. But that evening at Landover I had an elated sense of paying tribute to the game, the people, and the franchise that had given me so much.

Toward the end of the second quarter, as I sat on the bench after my second touchdown, I allowed myself to savor the moment. The Giants were winning and playing great. Normally during a game I focus entirely on the here and now. I'm in the zone. I don't hear the fans. I am not really registering where I am or what's going on beyond the playing field.

But for a quick moment during the Washington game, I let my guard slip. I relaxed and did something I never do, which was turn around and look into the stands from the bench.

Usually the insults rain down from the home-fan stands throughout the game. So there's no benefit, really, in even glancing toward the fans. But that night I allowed myself a good last look at a crowded stadium in full roar. I had a valedictory feeling. I was saying good-bye to all that.

As I gazed up into the stands, a dark-haired man in glasses stood up. He was about ten rows away from me. This was Washington fan territory, so I didn't expect anything from him except bile. But the dark-haired guy looked straight at me. It was odd, as though a moment was passing between us.

"Your father loves you," he said, distinctly and directly to me.

The hair on the back of my neck stood up. I had never seen him before and never have since. He could have been talking about Jesus, for all I knew. "Father" with a capital "F." He could have known my background and was looking to connect.

It didn't matter. I turned back around to follow the action on the field.

But his words stayed with me. The whole evening, the last regular-season game of my career, had naturally put me in a thoughtful, contemplative frame of mind. And then there came a message from the past, winging its way out of a crowd from the lips of a stranger.

Nothing's over, I thought. Despite the media buzz over my retirement, despite the helmet slaps and high fives of my teammates, despite my own feelings of leave-taking, I had a whole life ahead of me.

A decade earlier, my father had attended my last college game, when we played his old school team, Virginia Tech. We ended up losing. I didn't really have anything to say to him afterward. The meeting was awkward, because I hadn't spent time with him in so long.

After that brief encounter, I didn't see J.B. at all. He e-mailed me and sent me a card from time to time. I never responded. I didn't feel a connection to him. My father has two other children now, a boy and a girl in their mid-teens, my half brother and sister, both pretty good athletes. I'm pretty sure they're aware of who their half brother is, but we have never spoken.

I believe J.B. might be looking for peace in his life, or some sort of closure. That will come only with Ronde and me acknowledging James Barber as our father. I am not ready for that yet. I don't know if I will ever be ready.

But that day at Landover, my heart felt as though it were going to beat out of my chest. "Your father loves you."

Nothing's over. I've got a whole life ahead of me. And I've got a lot of work to do.

TIKI INTERVIEWS TIKI

Q What did you learn on one side of the microphone—as the subject of so many interviews and profiles—that you are now applying to the other side of the microphone as a reporter?

A Do my homework. Most reporters are principled, interesting people. A few are not, and I have learned there is absolutely no accountability if you're not, especially in sports. I've seen such sloppy and almost comically negligent journalism. It doesn't even qualify as reporting. It's more like creative lying, except it isn't that creative. They align their stories with their prejudices instead of with the facts. They have written the whole article in their minds before they ever talk to you, and nothing you can say will change it. I've been on interviews like that, and it can be a very surreal experience: It's as if your words just vanish into thin air. When I entered broadcasting a decade ago, I swore I would never do it that way. I would abide by a few rules I laid down for myself. Do my homework. Base my reporting on the facts. Leave my prejudices at home. Give my subject a fair shake, and give the story my best.

EPILOGUE

Hall of Fame quarterback Y. A. Tittle tells a story of how his career almost ended—and then did not. After nine seasons with San Francisco, Tittle saw the writing on the wall when the 49ers started to give up-and-coming QB John Brodie more and more playing time. Tittle was already thirty when San Francisco drafted Brodie in 1957.

In a preseason game against the Giants in 1961, Brodie started and played the whole first half. New York took Brodie apart, dominating the game. The 49ers put Tittle in as QB for the second half. Almost magically, the momentum turned around. Tittle had the game of his life. He dodged pass rushers and completed passes. He routed the Giants. *Maybe my career isn't over after all,* he thought.

The next day, he learned he had been traded . . . to the New York Giants. It turned out that one of the coaches for the Giants, so I'm told, had given the players a little heads-up before the game. If Tittle comes in, go easy on him, because he's going to be our quarterback this year. We want him in one piece.

Tittle went on to lead the Giants to three NFL championships. He was NFL MVP in 1963, at age thirty-seven. The next year he retired.

It's just a question of how you want to go out. Tittle chose to push his years of achievement. Barry Sanders left at the top of his game, weary of being the only great player on his team. Pete Sampras beat Andre Agassi to win the U.S. Open in 2002 at age thirty-one—and then retired.

In the midst of the screaming and shouting over my impending retirement, Curtis Martin quietly hobbled onto the injury list for the New York Jets. Curtis is one of the true greats of the game. His numbers are astonishing. His low-key personality allowed him to be chronically overlooked, but in any discussion of great running backs, his name should be mentioned right at the top.

The year 2006 was to be Martin's twelfth NFL season. But his knees failed him. In 2004 he had rushed for 1,697 yards. He hoped for one more good year. The news of his injury was buried in the sports section. Meanwhile, on the front pages and in many of the columns of that same section, writers fussed about the outlandish idea that I might retire of my own free choice. I saw Martin interviewed on sports broadcasts. The camera showed him limping painfully.

Is that how they want me to go off? Is that the only honorable way to leave the game?

Again, pardon the language, but fuck that.

Here's how I always wanted to go out: Intact, not damaged. Walking upright, not limping. I wanted the opponent in the last game of my career to be my old favorite team from childhood, the Redskins. I wanted the Giants to win, and with that win, enter the play-offs. And I wanted to have a ridiculous game, a career-high day.

Wait. That really happened.

Playing the game of football is over for me now. I know I did it proud—I "played proud," as my mom would say. My past—the Giants, the games, my fellow players—is receding quickly in all the activities of the present. But it's like the line they print on a car mirror: "Objects in the rearview mirror may be closer than they appear."

This is my life today, and *Today*: I'm in New York, the greatest city in the world. My utmost happiness comes from being with Ginny and watching our sons grow up. Getting AJ and Chason together with Ronde and his daughters—well, it doesn't get any better than that, especially when my mom is around too, and Ginny's parents.

I fielded some questions recently from a group of schoolkids as part of a program to promote reading. A fourth-grade girl sent in a question: "Did you ever think you would be a celebrity?"

I quoted Ralph Waldo Emerson to her in my reply: "Each man is a hero to somebody."

I told her I believed that no matter what your job was, if you did it well, you would be celebrated. I just happened to have a job that a lot of people wanted and that attracted a lot of attention. That's what made me a celebrity.

"A lot of people do their jobs well," I said in my reply. "Your mom and dad, your teacher—and they are justifiably celebrated too."

I've gone from one high-profile job to another, but it's more important for me to be a hero in the eyes of my sons than all the fan cheers and the Nielsens put together.

Today represents the network benchmark in morning television. I generate my own stories or work on assignments. The arrangement suits a restless, questing mind. The show fits me to a T, primarily because it is a fresh challenge.

I still get to keep one foot in football, with NBC's *Football Night in America*.

I don't have the patience for a lot of kinds of football analysis. It begins to sound inane to me. "Blah-blah and they're back to the 3–4 defense. You can see how that disrupted the offense." Who can listen to that? It's football-nerd talk.

Given the chaos and variables that play out on a football field, I've always believed pregame prognostication to be so much hot air. If anyone really knew anything about what was going to happen when two NFL teams meet, the sports betting industry wouldn't be a multi-billion-dollar sector of the economy.

But *Football Night*, which comes on before NBC's Sunday night NFL broadcast, is all about analyzing the games of the day *after* they happen, not before. That's always more interesting to me.

Beyond *Today* and *Football Night*, the peacock network also means the Olympics. I've been a fan all my life. For the Los Angeles games in 1984, I recall being riveted to the TV. I was nine years old, and that was when the dream to go to the Olympics probably first entered my head.

Courtesy of NBC, Jeff Zucker, and Dick Ebersol, my dream is going to come true, though not exactly in the way I imagined. I'm looking forward to covering the Beijing games in 2008 and the Vancouver games in 2010.

In fact, for 2008 I've already embarked on a new project: learning Mandarin Chinese. I'm not sure how much of the language I'll be able to absorb. Perhaps just enough to say "Hello" and "How are you?" But I'll give it my best shot.

你认为如何

What do you think about that?

APPENDIX: STATS

During the ten years (1997–2006) Tiki Barber played in the National Football League, no one racked up more all-purpose yards, combining rush, reception, and return yardage for a 17,359-yard total. He led the NFL in total yards from scrimmage in both 2004 and 2005.

Barber's career numbers place him among the elite backs in the history of the NFL. He retired as the game's seventeenth all-time leading rusher, tenth all-time in yards from scrimmage, third all-time in yards per carry at 4.7.

Barber is one of twenty-one players in NFL history to have rushed for more than 10,000 yards, and the first player to have more than 1,800 rushing yards and more than 500 receiving yards in the same season. His 2,390 yards from scrimmage 2005 season is the second most of all time. He ranks with Marshall Faulk and Marcus Allen as the only three players to gain more than 10,000 yards rushing and more than 5,000 receiving, and he joins Faulk in having four 2,000-total-yard seasons.

In 2006 the Pro Football Hall of Fame in Canton, Ohio, requested Barber's December 30, 2006, game jersey to honor his NFL records for most yards rushing in a running back's last season (1,662 yards), and most yards in a running back's last game (234 rushing yards and 258 all-purpose yards versus the Washington Redskins).

Barber holds a host of Giants team records. On January 2, 2005, in the 2004 season finale at home versus the Dallas Cowboys, Barber broke both Rodney Hampton's Giants' all-time rushing record and Joe Morris's single-season rushing record. He has the most rushing touchdowns (fifty-five) of any Giant. His ninety-five-yard touchdown on December 31, 2005, against the Oakland Raiders is the team record for the longest scoring run from scrimmage. From 2002 to 2006, he was the Giants' rushing leader for eighty consecutive games, an NFL record. He retired from the Giants as the team's all-time leader in both rushing and receiving.

RUSHING

Year	G	GS	Att	Yds	Avg	Lg	TD	20+	1st
1997	12	6	136	511	3.8	42	3	2	31
1998	16	4	52	166	3.2	23	0	1	8
1999	16	1	62	258	4.2	30	0	1	12
2000	16	12	213	1,006	4.7	78	8	9	38
2001	14	9	166	865	5.2	36	4	8	40
2002	16	15	304	1,387	4.6	70	11	12	67
2003	16	16	278	1,216	4.4	27	2	4	66
2004	16	14	322	1,518	4.7	72	13	11	77
2005	16	16	357	1,860	5.2	95	9	16	72
2006	16	16	327	1,662	5.1	55	5	11	78
TOTAL	154	109	2,217	10,449	4.7	95	55	75	489

APPENDIX: STATS

RECEIVING

Year	Rec	Yds	Avg	Lg	TD	20+	40+	1st
1997	34	299	8.8	29	1	2	0	13
1998	42	348	8.3	87	3	3	1	13
1999	66	609	9.2	56	2	6	1	32
2000	70	719	10.3	36	1	10	0	29
2001	72	577	8.0	44	0	4	1	30
2002	69	597	8.7	38	0	5	0	23
2003	69	461	6.7	36	1	3	0	26
2004	52	578	11.1	62	2	8	3	18
2005	54	530	9.8	48	2	5	1	19
2006	58	465	8.0	28	0	2	0	23
TOTAL	586	5,183	8.8	87	12	48	7	226

KICK RETURNS

Year	G	No	Yds	Avg	Lg	TD	40+
1997	12	0	0	—	0	0	0
1998	16	14	250	17.9	32	0	0
1999	16	12	266	22.2	41	0	1
2000	16	1	28	28.0	28	0	0
TOTAL	60	27	544	20.1	41	0	1

PUNT RETURNS

Year	G	Ret	FC	Ret Yds	Avg	Lg	TD	20+
1999	16	44	13	506	11.5	85	1	6
2000	16	39	20	332	8.5	31	0	3
2001	14	38	12	338	8.9	23	0	4
2002	16	1	1	5	5.0	5	0	0
TOTAL	62	122	46	1,181	9.7	85	1	13

FUMBLES

Year	Fum	Lost	Own Rec	Opp Rec	Yds	Tot Rec	TD
1997	3	1	0	0	0	0	0
1998	1	0	0	0	0	0	0
1999	5	0	5	0	0	5	0
2000	9	3	5	0	0	5	0
2001	8	2	6	0	2	6	0
2002	9	6	1	0	0	1	0
2003	9	6	4	0	0	4	0
2004	5	2	2	0	0	2	0
2005	1	1	1	0	0	1	0
2006	3	1	1	0	0	1	0
TOTAL	53	22	25	0	2	25	0

UNIVERSITY OF VIRGINIA CAVALIERS (1993–1996)

- All-purpose yards: 4,883
- Rushing yards/attempts/average: 3,389/651/5.2
- 100+ rushing games: 19
- 1000+ rushing seasons: 2 (1995 and 1996)

ACKNOWLEDGMENTS

The efforts of a lot of people went into the making of this book, including everyone at Simon & Schuster: Jack Romanos, whose editorial insights are as on target as his golf game; my publisher, Jen Bergstrom, and my editor, Tricia Boczkowski, who shepherded this book to completion; and my collaborator, Gil Reavill, who took my words and made a book out of them.

Thanks to Mark Lepselter, who was a prime motivator on this project and in my life. You've always been a friend, ally, and fellow warrior in all that I've done. Also, without the mentors I've been privileged to have over the years, this book would not be possible, so to all of those on whose shoulders I've stood along my journey, who have inspired me, motivated me, and taught me to be my own man; from every coach to every teacher to every friend I've grown to know, thank you: I am a product of all of you. And finally, to my twin brother, Ronde; I love you for always telling me what I need to hear and not just what I want to hear.

YOU'LL SCORE

with these other great books
by NFL superstars
Tiki and Ronde Barber

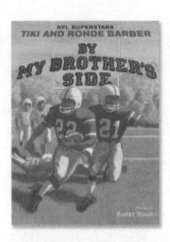

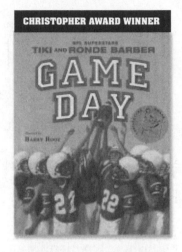

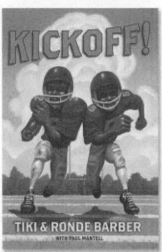

To learn more visit www.simonsayskids.com

From Paula Wiseman Books • Published by Simon & Schuster